Doctor Who: Episode-by-Episode

Volume 7 – Sylvester McCoy

(Unofficial and Unauthorised)

By Ray Dexter

A Spinderella Paperback

First published in Great Britain in 2015

By Spinderella

1 2 3 4 5 6 7 8 9 10 11 12

ISBN: 978-1-326-54096-8

Doctor Who: Episode-by-Episode

Volume 7 – Sylvester McCoy

(Unofficial and Unauthorised)

By Ray Dexter

For Aron and Maja, as always.

The first *Doctor Who* story Ray Dexter can remember watching is *The Ribos Operation*. His favourite story is *Inferno*. This is his 11th book.

All contact by readers is welcome, especially for the proposed New Adventures Volume. Please use Twitter:

@ray_dexter

Thanks must go to: Andy 'Witchmark' Hunt, Jerome Jones and Richard Saunders for their helpful comments.

Appreciation must go out to Andrew Pixley, David J Howe, Stephen James Walker and Mark Stammers for their incredible work without whom no book on *Doctor Who* can be written.

Introduction

This is the seventh of a series of books on watching *Doctor Who*. Why do we need another *Doctor Who* book? In simple terms it's because everybody watches it the wrong way. Ever since the widespread availability of video cassette recorders and their subsequently more advanced offspring, fans of the show have been able to watch *Doctor Who* whenever they want and in whatever order they want. In addition, since the 1966 story *The Savages*, when individual episode titles gave way to an umbrella title for a whole adventure, there has been an assumption that *Doctor Who* was a show about self-contained stories rather than an evolving narrative. The return of the show in 2005, with its re-introduced format of individual episodes was a clever return to the original premise of *Doctor Who* and also frustrating for fans who want the proper title for a story, not something like *Hell Bent/Heaven Sent*. Under Steven Moffat the show has barely paid lip service to conventional structured stories and instead has carried through threads and plotlines through whole eras.

This series of books chronicle the show episode-by-episode. In so doing it allows the reader the opportunity to follow the developments of the character known as the Doctor in the order they were created and in the process, highlighting some of the inconsistencies created by new teams taking on the job of making the show. If you are any kind of *Doctor Who* fan I do urge you to find the time one year* to watch your favourite show, in order, from the start.

The understanding and the deep love for the programme fostered will make it all worth it.

(*That's funny, I started watching in 2012 and I finished in November 2015!)

A note on watching Doctor Who

One of the frustrating things about being a *Doctor Who* fan is the 100 or so missing Episodes from the archive. As such, you cannot 'watch' *Doctor Who* from start to finish. There are gaps in the fossil record. Up until the late 1970s the BBC had a 'save video tape' policy and all episodes bar a few random examples kept for the archive were wiped to reuse the tape. This went on all the way through the Jon Pertwee era too. Fortunately black and white film copies for overseas export were made and many of these survived, but 97 Episodes have been lost forever. Even more fortunately, from the beginning there had always been *Doctor Who* fans who recorded the audio soundtrack off the speaker on their televisions. This means that we can hear all the missing episodes – miraculous really. Another piece of luck was that a man called John Cura invented a technique called 'telesnaps', where he would take small but good quality photographs of the episodes as they were broadcast on a television screen, giving interested parties a record of the show for a fee. He did a lot of work on *Doctor Who*, but not every episode was 'telesnapped'. Since the 1980s when these telesnaps were rediscovered fans have been marrying the tape's soundtracks (now beautifully restored and with linking narration, thanks to the BBC) to Cura's telesnaps to make slide-show versions of the missing episodes. They're not perfect but they are better than nothing. Many are available these days on the *You Tube* web page and have taken these reconstructions out of the hands of the underground fan scene. Some are very good indeed and the technology and dedication has come so far that some fans have created good versions of episodes where no telesnaps exist at all – a major problem during the final Hartnell stories, and any from after Cura's death in 1968. Technically the BBC could get annoyed with such copyright breaking reconstructions but, perhaps because of their guilt at the destruction of the episodes in first place, the painstaking work to put them together and the fact that they are non-profit making and done for love, they turn a blind eye. In fact they have used similar techniques themselves on some VHS releases. So, with the various media and access to *You Tube* you can now 'watch' every episode of *Doctor Who*.

None of this really affects you at this stage in the *Doctor Who* story. All the Seventh Doctor stories exist, and all *Doctor Who* stories have been released on DVD.

A word about the categories

Although *Doctor Who* can be thought of as episodic, each 'story' had its own assigned writers and directors and guest stars and as such it is convenient to block them this way. Each story therefore has its own categories. They are detailed below.

Title
Very easy here, as each story has a name on screen. It wasn't so easy for the Hartnell era and won't be easy when we get to 2005. Enjoy the simplicity while it is simple!

Availability
At the time of writing how can you 'see' this story?

One line summary
An attempt to give you a quick synopsis.

Key Players
Actors who play the significant characters in the show making their debuts. This can open up another can of worms, especially in this edition. For the purposes of this book I am including the recurring actor who played the Master and the two voice artists who played K9.

Producer, Script Editor, Director, Writer
The main creative team behind the show. Where they make their first appearance you will find a brief biography.

<u>Anything else before we start?</u>
This section fills you in with some of the behind the scenes facts about the production.

<u>The Episodes</u>
This is the most free-form aspect of the book. It's essentially anything that springs to mind as I watched the episode. Sometimes this takes the form of plot; this is especially true in missing episodes, where the subtleties of the story may not be known to the reader. In more well-known stories this may take the form of extended comments on how the story plays out and other things worth noting. Each episode starts with a briefly summary in italics from the *Radio Times'* listing blurb. Up to five asterisks will be by the Episode number giving my rating for the episode.

<u>Verdict</u>
This is my opinion of the story as watched in order.

<u>Other famous reviews</u>
Over the years there have been many books analysing and reviewing every *Doctor Who* story. Some were written by very famous *Doctor Who* fans, others by relative unknowns. This section is an attempt to provide a flavour of the opinions of the story and perhaps give the conventional view if it differs from my take on it.

Ratings
The average viewing figures for the whole of the story. If any particular episode had a very high or very low rating this will also be noted.

Chart positions
This is a less well-known set of data but it is the current measure of new *Doctor Who*. This is the average chart position for the story and, given the huge differences in audience figures between successful shows in the 1960s and now, it gives perhaps a better perspective to exactly how popular the show was in relation to other shows of the time. The figure in brackets takes the chart position this story received and rates it against other *Doctor Who* stories, thus providing a list of the highest charting *Doctor Who* stories (*Voyage of the Damned, Journey's End, The Next Doctor*) through to the lowest (*The Curse of Fenric* – which didn't appear to chart at all). A full list will appear in the final edition of these books.

Position in the Mighty 200 poll
Doctor Who Magazine celebrated the reaching of 200 *Doctor Who* stories by asking readers to vote for their favourite stories. This is the position this story came in that list. Since these books were started there has been a fiftieth anniversary poll. The newer results appears in brackets. There is no significant change.

What have we discovered?
Again, anything new or anything pithy that can be said about the story is written here.

The story so far…on screen.

On the 22nd November 1963 two teachers from Coal Hill School, London (Ian and Barbara) go beyond the call of duty with regards to a strange pupil called Susan. She is a brilliant scientist and a sometimes brilliant historian, but in other ways she shows huge ignorance. They follow her to a junk yard where they have an uncomfortable encounter with her cantankerous old Grandfather, who spirits them away in a police box significantly bigger on the inside than out. The old man is called the Doctor and he cannot control this box his granddaughter calls TARDIS. They have a series of adventures, some set in the future, some set in Earth's past, some in 'sideways' worlds.

Early on they encounter some vicious aliens called Daleks. After one particularly harrowing adventure in Earth's future, where our heroes over-turn a Dalek invasion of Earth almost single-handedly Susan leaves, having fallen in love with a member of the anti-Dalek resistance. Ian and Barbara continue to travel with the Doctor, becoming less angry at their abductor and more excited by the possibilities open to them to see the universe. However, after a particularly weird adventure on the Planet Vortis their enthusiasm perhaps wanes a little and after an adventure where the Daleks chase them through time and space they take the opportunity to return to Earth in an abandoned Dalek time machine. The Doctor continues to travel with a variety of younger companions. We also discover another person from the same planet as him. In his last adventure the First Doctor, having been subjected to a variety of very draining procedures over the previous set of adventures, collapses, having been present at an attempt by metal creatures called Cybermen to drain the Earth of all its energy. As the credits close the old man's face turns into a much younger one.

This younger version of the Doctor was much more playful than the previous incarnation. He had an early obsession with hats and a lifelong obsession with his recorder. He soon met his most iconic companion Jamie and they had a series of rather 'Earth in the future' style stories against a series of horrific monsters, the most famous being the Cybermen. Eventually, in an adventure where a race of people used thousands of Earth soldiers to fight wars the Doctor calls in his own people, the Time Lords to help out. He is put on trial and it is revealed that he ran away from his people and stole the TARDIS. He is found guilty, exiled to Earth and given a new face.

The Third Doctor is a dashing, rather upper-class sort of character who simultaneously hates his exile on Earth, while paradoxically fitting in very well indeed. This version of the Doctor is happy to name-drop his own planet and its people all of a sudden, and the Time Lords become much more invasive in his life than before. In many ways this is a good thing, as Earth is subject to a huge amount of invasions in this era. The Doctor hooks up with UNIT, which he met in his previous incarnation and becomes their Scientific Advisor, with an ever-changing laboratory that he can use to try and fix his TARDIS. The 'UNIT family' as it was known become a regular feature of his adventures, and his muscle in times of trouble. During his time on Earth his arch-Time Lord nemesis, the Master returns to his life and carries out a series of rather convoluted plots to gain power. He also has trouble with reptile-like creatures who once lived on the planet, who believe the planet should rightfully be theirs.

The Doctor gradually gets more freedom to travel, but it is usually with the Time Lords' blessing, until Omega, a Time Lord from the old times, a hero who died to provide the power the Time Lords live by, is found alive and well and going insane in an anti-matter world. The Time Lords, faced with a collapsing universe, summon the Doctor's previous two incarnations to help fight Omega. Their success leads to the Doctor getting his freedom to travel in his TARDIS again.

A series of adventures follow where the Doctor fails to take his latest companion Jo Grant to Metebelis 3. Ultimately this leads to the Third Doctor having a crisis of Buddhist contemplation upon meeting a giant spider on Metebelis 3 and virtually sacrificing his 'self' for the story.

The Doctor regenerates again into a very tall eccentric Bohemian man who gradually severs his connections with UNIT and yearns to travel the universe. He encounters a series of grizzly villains and the creator of the Daleks, Davros. His ability to show great anger and great charm makes him a formidable adversary. Initially he travels with Sarah Jane Smith but after he is called back to his home planet she is ditched on Earth. On Gallifrey the Doctor is accused of murdering the President but after a brutal battle in the Matrix, the collected knowledge bank of the Time Lords, the Doctor realises his true enemy is a horribly mutated Master. Surviving this the Doctor finds a savage as a companion and tries to teach her to be civilised.

9

After his adventures on Gallifrey the Doctor seems to feel he is untouchable and he embarks on a series of adventures where he jokes and quips his way through, barely drawing sweat. He even manages to find the six segments of the Key to Time, a device the Guardians of the Universe use to keep it in balance. After even the Black Guardian can't defeat him he gets even more egotistical. With an equally know-it-all companion, fellow Time Lord Romana, and a know-it-all tin dog called K9 they become almost insufferable. Then, something happens...

We don't know what precisely as it's not seen on screen but the Doctor returns for a final series of adventures in a burgundy stylised uniform. The wise cracks and flippancy are gone. He seems to have aged and seems weary. He starts to pick up a series of younger companions: Adric, Tegan, and Nyssa, the latter who discovers her father's body has been snatched by the Master in need of a new body. Finally, as the Master tries to run the universe by destroying Logopolis the Doctor falls to his death from a giant telescope.

The new incarnation is a much younger, vulnerable man. Here we have an incarnation that seems to doubt his ability to solve problems. His companions don't help, being moany and whiney and seeming to not really want to go on adventures. He seems exasperated by them. After an adventure against the Cybermen Adric sacrifices himself and dies. The Doctor seems haunted by this for the rest of his incarnation; in fact his last words will be 'Adric'. The Black Guardian returns to get revenge and puts a treacherous companion Turlough onto the TARDIS, who nearly succeeds in killing the Doctor. Again the Guardian is thwarted, only for seemingly every foe the Doctor has encountered before to line up to attack him: Daleks, Silurians, Sea Devils, Omega: all beaten. There is even time for another Gallifrey plot which puts all five of his incarnations up against a fellow Time Lord's quest for immortality. Finally, on Androzani Major, with both him and new companion Peri dying from spectrox toxaemia he barely survives a brutal mud-spattered adventure. Peri is saved; but the Doctor is forced to regenerate. Up sits an arrogant, curly- haired man.

This new Doctor quotes Shakespeare and asserts his academic superiority on most of the universe, and Peri in particular, who seems terrified of him. To complement his brash personality this incarnation dons a horribly garish costume and marches around quite alien locales looking for trouble. Although actually rarely in trouble this Doctor is unfriendly but paradoxically seems to have more old friends in the universe than other Doctors – especially ones we haven't met before.

Precisely how long-lasting this incarnation was is difficult to be sure of as his time-line was interfered with horribly by the Time Lords, in particular one called the Valeyard. The Doctor was plucked out of time after a horrific adventure on Thoros Beta where (and again it's difficult to be certain) the Doctor behaved poorly and Peri was killed to provide a body for slug-like creature called Kiv. Once plucked out of time the Doctor was put on trial for his continued meddling in the affairs of others although ironically the trial itself was a farce designed to cover up the meddling of the Time Lords in Earth's history. The Valeyard turns out to be a future incarnation of the Doctor. Although the Doctor escapes this trial and has at least one other adventure – one we see through the prism of the Trial - he goes on to have a new companion called Mel, who he never actually meets but who he takes with him before he meets her – I know, I know. Finally, to add to the confusion the Rani pulls the TARDIS out of time and the Doctor hits his head which seems to cause another regeneration...

The story so far...off screen.

Remember that saying about a camel being a horse designed by a committee? The implication being of course that committees always make a mess of things. *Doctor Who* is the perfect riposte to this argument and shows that committees can produce brilliant work. In fact it can be argued that *Doctor Who*'s lasting success is almost entirely due to nobody owning the idea, nobody over-ruling others, simply a lot of hired hands doing a job. Andrew Pixley has unearthed documents that show that in 1962 the BBC commissioned a report on the feasibility of 'science fiction' programmes from two story editors, Donald Bull and Alice Frick. Their conclusion seems to have been that little science fiction was good for television, as viewers preferred action adventures. A further report from Frick and another colleague John Braybon suggested science fiction books with good characterization, no bug eyed monsters and low demand for special effects. Fast forward to March 26th 1963 and Sydney Newman, a Canadian recently appointed as Head of Drama and Serials, held a meeting with Frick, Braybon, Donald

Wilson (Head of Serials) and 'Bunny' Webber, (a BBC staff writer) to discuss a possible science fiction series to fill the early Saturday evening slot. A brain storm seems to have given various ideas, including a space/time machine, scientific trouble shooters and the need for various identification characters, including a 'maturer man,' with some 'character twist.' Newman gave the maturer man the 'fled from his own world in a time machine' twist. Webber took these ideas and came up with a proposal he called *Doctor Who*. How all these ideas eventually made it to screen could take another book, but this is the essence of the matter.

The show was given to a young producer, Verity Lambert. She was Roedean and Sorbonne educated, and became Sydney Newman's production assistant having been promoted from a typist's position. Described as 'full of piss and vinegar' by Newman she had never produced nor directed before, but with Newman's backing she was given the job, despite some rumblings from the more establishment figures at the BBC. She went on to produce some equally great shows including *Minder* and *Jonathan Creek*. Newman credits her as 'the one who realized it all' – as great a compliment as you can get. Lambert, along with experienced script writer David Whitaker created the show as we know it. She was responsible for casting William Hartnell as the Doctor.

All the great plans for education and no bug-eyed monsters fell apart though when the Daleks took off in a big way in the second story. *Doctor Who*'s popularity continued to increase to a ratings peak of 13.5 million viewers with a story called *The Web Planet*, by which time a blue print for the

13

show had been established where stories would be either in the future, past or sideways. Writers known to be particularly skilled in one area or another were hired to write typical stories. Lambert left essentially after two seasons and was replaced by a man called John Wiles. Wiles struggled to leave his mark on the show and argued terribly with Hartnell. Wiles resigned mid-way through Season Three to be replaced by Innes Lloyd. Hartnell's health was failing and the ratings had sunk to an all-time low. Lance Parkin ascribes this fall to the success of *Batman* on ITV. Hartnell was replaced and Lloyd concluded that the only stories worth doing were ones with monsters. All he had to do now then cast a new person to play the Doctor. He managed it with aplomb, and Patrick Troughton carried on in the role, apparently playing a younger version of the same Doctor.

The new Doctor soon acquires his iconic companion Jamie, played by Frazer Hines. Innes Lloyd's other great innovation was to spend big money on a huge set and this type of *Who* adventure dominated the first two years of Troughton's reign. The type of story became known amongst fans as 'base-under-siege'. By Troughton's third season the wheels were falling off. None of the production team really wanted to be running the show and the stories become much more variable in tone and quality. This had an effect on the viewers and there was some discussion about whether the show had run its course. With colour television coming in and no extra money to make the show the idea of Earth-bound adventures in a 26-week series firmed up. Troughton wanted to leave too so Derrick Sherwin and Peter Bryant, somewhat reluctantly in charge at the time, cast Jon Pertwee and prepared to hand over the reins to someone who *did* want to be producer: a certain Barry Letts.

There followed a period of stability in *Doctor Who*. Dicks and Letts remained with the show for an unprecedented (up to then) five years, as did Jon Pertwee. The show shook off some of its starchy, futuristic Earth-in-crisis appearance of the first season and became a more matey reflection of Letts' world view and his religious beliefs. Buddhism and spiritual ideas became very popular indeed and the ratings soared. The show embraced colour and a new effects technique called Colour Separation Overlay, which at its best allowed lots of great effects, but at its worse was used to save money on sets. After five years the show was on a high when Pertwee, Letts and Dicks all felt it was time to move on...

The new production team were Philip Hinchcliffe and Robert Holmes. Together they were absolutely determined to produce the best *Doctor Who* they could. They managed it. For three years they made gripping television, admittedly the roots were showing. We got *Frankenstein*, shape shifters, and other B-movie rip offs, but it worked so well. The horror was cranked up and this would be their undoing. One horror shot too many though caused Hinchcliffe to be moved to another project and humour being pushed instead.

The new producer was Graham Williams. He had many problems: inflation meant the money wouldn't go as far, *Star Wars* was raising the bar, and Tom Baker was proving increasingly difficult to manage, ad libbing like crazy. His script editor was Anthony Read, a classicist who liked to add Greek Mythology to stories and the umbrella concept of the Key to Time was a welcome innovation. By Season 17 came along Douglas Adams was script editor and the silliness was starting to overwhelm.

Williams resigned when he couldn't stand Baker anymore and in came the Production Manager John Nathan-Turner. He created a whole new feel to the show. New theme, new titles, new costume. And within a year, a new lead actor too. The Nathan-Turner era was a new (and perhaps false) dawn; the early stories had a modern, ethereal quality never seen before, but this early promise soon disappeared as reviving monsters proved very popular to an increasingly vocal hard-core fan base, who the producer listened to increasingly. His script editor was Eric Saward, a man who liked macho stories about mercenaries and the show pushed a violent, confusing agenda with gaudy guest stars, returning monsters and over-lit sets. The returning Robert Holmes penned the last story of the Davison era and pushed the envelope as far as it would go, or so we thought.

Summarising the messy behind the scenes politics of the Colin Baker era is an impossible job, suffice to say that all the problems that had been brewing for years came to a head and the show was cancelled by the controller of BBC television, Michael Grade. A huge protest, led by the Producer gave it a temporary reprieve and the show came back for a limp 14-episode second chance. By then the producer and Script editor bother didn't want to be there but could find no escape route. The planned *Trial of a Time Lord* season was marred by the death of Robert Holmes and an increasingly upset Saward, who resigned before the season was completed and refused to let the team use his material.

The final episode was written in a hurry by Pip and Jane Baker and Colin Baker was fired. As we leave the Colin Baker era the show has never been less popular or more likely to die...

Season 24

Time and the Rani

One Line Summary: Hi John, Jonathan Powell here, no I'm not going to move you on and yes we've decided to recommission *Doctor Who*. Yes I know I've given you no notice but I don't want it to be good, do I? What do you mean you expected this and have a script ready just in case? Drat, drat, drat!

Producer: John Nathan-Turner - Midlands born, as plain old John Turner – the Nathan was added in 1968 when he needed to change his name because actors' union Equity already had a John Turner registered. 'Nathan' was more stylish too, according to a reference in his most recent biography. He had worked as an extra in the 1960s before become a floor assistant on *Doctor Who*: first on *The Space Pirates*, then *Ambassadors of Death* and *Colony in Space*. He and *Doctor Who* met again when he became Production Unit Manager for the show in 1976. Given his skilful handling of the budgets in previous seasons he was offered the promotion to Producer after Graham Williams left in late 1979. He produced the rest of the Classic Series' run, often against his will. While this book has been in preparation a new biography about Nathan-Turner was released by Richard Marson. In the wake of the Jimmy Savile revelations the chapter about Nathan-Turner and his partner Gary Downie's rather predatory attitude to young men, including Marson himself briefly put *Doctor Who* back on the front pages of the UK tabloids newspapers in 2013. Marson, an early features writer on *Doctor Who Magazine* and latterly editor of *Blue Peter*, is a reliable source, and this book been a valued reference as back-up the material in this book. The book is worth a read, although the story is a very sad one in lots of ways.

John Nathan-Turner was the longest-serving and the most infamous producer of *Doctor Who*. He is also the personality who divides opinion more than any other, but irrespective of your opinion of the show under his watch, it cannot be denied that his sheer persistence saved the show from cancellation in 1985. By the time he came to the events in this book he desperately wanted to move on to other projects, but the BBC had other ideas...

Script Editor: Andrew Cartmel - described at the time by Nathan-Turner as simply a young man in his 20s; he thought Cartmel's work was 'smashing.' When they first met they had a 'sparky' conversation. This, according to McCoy consisted of Cartmel's answering to the question: "What do you want to achieve in Doctor Who?" with, "Overthrow the government!"

Either way Nathan-Turner decided to hire him on the spot, but did point out that overthrowing the government was unlikely and that he'd more likely be discussing how black, white, green and purple people can actually get on.

In his amazon.com biography he describes his time on *Doctor Who* as 'legendary'. With a quarter of his output in the bottom ten, as rated both by fans in surveys and viewers who actually tuned in, this could be considered rather self-aggrandising to the average fan. However, as we'll see, he does have a point...

New cast: The Doctor: Sylvester McCoy - Born Percy Kent Smith in Scotland 1943 he trained as a priest at Blair's College, a seminary in Aberdeen up until the age of 16. From there he decided to become a monk, but was too young and was sent to a grammar school instead. It was there that he discovered girls and decided against religion. According to him he had his heart broken by one of the girls (Elswyth Calder) so he went on holiday to London and kind of stayed. Looking back he feels he was attracted to the theatre of priesthood rather than the spiritual.

His flit to London meant he ended up working in insurance. He enjoyed theatre and started working at the Roundhouse Theatre in North London as a ticket collector. There, whilst the queues queued he started improvising with another actor, Brian Murphy. Murphy assumed he was an actor and recommended him to Ken Campbell, who was starting his Ken Campbell's Roadshow troupe. Others in the troupe included Bob

Hoskins. For one show he used the name Sylveste McCoy and a played a stuntman. This is where I have to mention nails up the nose and stuffing ferrets down his trousers. It's a contractual obligation. Over time McCoy drifted into straight theatre work and became a semi-famous face on children's television. According to Pixley he applied for the Sixth Doctor role in 1983. When asked by *Starlog* magazine what the new Doctor will be like he replied, 'he'll be a little smaller.'

Existing cast: Mel Bonnie Langford Mel – Bonnie Langford - Born Bonita Melody Lysette Langford in 1964 she had won *Opportunity Knocks* by the time she was six! She had starred on Broadway by the time she was fifteen, and the West End too. She was probably (tragically) remembered for her perhaps too-good performance of Violet Elizabeth Bott in the TV show *Just William* and many of my generation can still say (with horror) 'I'll scweem and scweem until I'm sick.' She was synonymous with dance shows and all that was ghastly about musicals and showbiz at the time of her casting and so was right up Nathan-Turner's street. She remains the most controversial appointment ever, just shading Catherine Tate.

Written by: Pip and Jane Baker - They met very young at a Labour Party meeting. According to Pixley: they were known to Nathan-Turner's predecessor Graham Williams because they had worked on the same shows

(*Z Cars, The Double Dealers*). Williams had wanted them to write for *Doctor Who* but they declined and claimed to have only ever seen the first episode in 1963 and had no idea of its cult following. Nathan-Turner found a script of theirs, *The Zodiac Factor* lying around the office, contacted them to see if they had changed their mind and wanted to write for the show. They didn't, they were more interested in creating new ideas. Nathan-Turner was clearly persistent however. Previous Script Editor Eric Saward didn't care for them at all and neither, as we'll see did Andrew Cartmel.

Directed by: Andrew Morgan - Born in Somerset, he spent two years at RADA before deciding to move into directing. He got a job as a holiday relief assistant floor manager at the BBC and stayed. Eventually, you guessed it, he completed the director's course. He had worked on *Blake's 7* before this and had been approached to direct *Timeflight*, but had successfully dodged that bullet.

Anything else before we start?
After the traumatic events surrounding the cancellation in 1985 and the subsequent behind-the-scenes debacle that was Season 23 (See Volume 6) which led to the firing of Colin Baker Nathan-Turner took extensive leave from the BBC. On his return he expected to never be involved with *Doctor Who* again. He was wrong. In truth the bosses didn't want the show but couldn't think

of what to replace it with and certainly didn't want another producer, or have Nathan Turner produce anything else, so he found himself back in the hot seat, having been 'persuaded to stay.'

Along comes Andrew Cartmel. As I've noted he had been working for a computer software company in Cambridge but he had ambitions as a writer. More importantly Cartmel wanted to make *Doctor Who* good again. "I was working in Cambridge at a computer company. I'd never previously really had a proper job, I'd always been writing, waiting to be successful as a writer. After my Dad died, I thought, 'Time's moving on, I can't just sit around writing; I've got to get a civilised, decent job.' So in the course of about three phone calls I organised a postgraduate thing in computer science which led to me getting a job a year later in Cambridge."

"I was very happy in Cambridge. It was a very groovy company full of ex-hippy vegetarians, designing incredible software of a kind I'd never seen. CAD stuff - Computer Aided Design. So I was beavering away there when I got a phone call from my agent. One thing I had achieved while I was starving as a writer in my garret was being invited to (the BBC had a thing called) the Script Unit, which would read unsolicited scripts and encourage writers - well, I used to be called in to their writer's workshops, with a bunch of other hopeful writers. A lot of whom, I have to say, have gone on to be very successful, often after being commissioned by me!

23

There was Ian Briggs, Malcolm Kohll, and Robin Mukherjee, although Robin never wrote for *Who*.

So, essentially we had a new young scriptwriter with lots of new contacts for people desperate to write for television. Also Nathan-Turner got on well with Cartmel and was relieved that he had a script editor who seemed to be able to work on his own to produce good scripts – something Nathan-Turner was never sure about. Perhaps part of the reason for the ultimate success of the partnership was that they didn't socialise, unlike Saward and Nathan-Turner.

The first job was to cast a new Doctor after Colin Baker made it clear he wouldn't return for one story. Casting McCoy was done properly this time after the 'wedding guest life and soul of the party moment' last time. There were screen tests and practice scenes. Director Andrew Morgan recalls that the final four were McCoy, Chris Jury (Deadbeat in The greatest show in the Galaxy), Ken Campbell and Dermot Crowley (who?) who Morgan felt was very good. McCoy felt Campbell would have made a better villain. McCoy's agent had rung up Nathan-Turner to say he was interested, Nathan-Turner had fobbed him off, but then Clive Doig, a producer who had worked with McCoy also rang up Nathan-Turner and the wheels began to turn. Nathan-Turner went to see McCoy in *The Pied Piper* at the National Theatre and McCoy felt it was a perfect audition piece (bright coat). McCoy *was* worried about being type cast, about knowing what he was going to be doing for the next few years.

Cartmel made extensive notes of his time on the show and were published in his book *Script Doctor*. Here Cartmel notes that the BBC bosses always decided at the 11th hour whether to re-commission the show and as such script commissions were very last minute. Nathan-Turner had covered himself by commissioning Pip and Jane Baker. The Bakers suggested the Rani rematch. And while Colin Baker was still technically the Doctor or thought persuadable to do a regeneration story the Rani was suggested as a suitable swansong villain. By coincidence Kate O'Mara, who played the Rani two seasons ago claims to have written to Nathan-Turner from sunny Hollywood saying "I can't stand the eternal sunshine…You've got to help me. I want to be in a gravel pit somewhere in the pissing rain, changing in a caravan in front of 20 nosey crewmembers."

The Bakers said that Nathan-Turner wanted a new monster and a giant brain and revamped a storyline they had used for a 'make your own adventure' book published in 1986. It's called *Race Against Time* (£7.50 on EBay if you're a completist). The Bakers even claimed to have phoned Colin Baker to persuade him to come back, to no avail. Nathan-Turner felt the story was interesting, if not highly complex with lots for O'Mara to do. The native Lakertyans were named after the Latin word Lacertian (lizard like). Originally called *Strange Matter* this was retitled *Time and the Rani* when Nathan-Turner wanted the Rani in the title. It plays on *Time and the Conways* by J. B Priestley (look, you ask them!)

The Bakers weren't so keen on McCoy, feeling he was too jokey; the spoons went too far for them, although McCoy enjoyed the opportunity to play them on O'Mara's décolletage. "Where would a Time Lord learn to play the bloody spoons?" moaned Pip. McCoy admitted to veering towards the Troughton portrayal which is often distilled down to 'jokey' in the folk memory. The costume was too loud for McCoy's taste and the 'choosing the costume' scene went on too long, again the Bakers deny their involvement. The costume itself was designed by Ken Trew and was based on golfing costumes of the 1930s (minus the question marks – which were the Nathan-Turner flourish).

The Bakers weren't keen on new boy Cartmel either. From their point of view they were seasoned veterans so in interviews they turned their noses up (saying things like Pip's brother had turned Cartmel down for a job at an aeronautics factory – so?). Cartmel acknowledged their work was structurally sound, but it was miles away from his vision.

You see Cartmel came from a world where comics were kin. His heroes were Alan Moore, especially titles such as *Swamp Thing*, hardly the Bakers' territory. Cartmel hated the Bakers' work because it had characters using words like 'Earthling' and 'incompetent fool' - he wasn't wrong. During one

26

meeting Cartmel tried to explain his reservations to the pair, but unfortunately let slip he was on a training course later in the day which Jane Baker 'shrieked "training" with venomous pleasure.' He did get his way in replacing the Bakers' choice of a genius (Solomon!) with Einstein, but their heart wasn't in it and he was not used very well. There were various conferences about the script between Nathan-Turner director Morgan, Cartmel and the Bakers which were slightly tense, let's say and if Cartmel had been in the job longer he would have removed them.

The regeneration scene is famous for all the wrong reasons. Morgan wanted a clip of Baker but that was vetoed, apparently by Nathan-Turner, so instead we saw McCoy in a blond, curly wig. McCoy claimed later that he had no idea Baker had been sacked and only thought things were a bit odd when they asked him to don the wig. While we're on the early regeneration stuff, the aphorism mix ups were mainly ad libbed, and the early Doctor eccentric scene was written by Cartmel to establish eccentricity. The Einstein kidnap scene was also added at Cartmel's request, although the Bakers were less impressed. McCoy took credit for the rolled rrrrrs.

The Rani's impersonation of Mel is notorious too. The Bakers justified it by noting that it should have been seriously played, but O'Mara found it terribly difficult to play to Langford's idiosyncrasies while she was also on set. Langford thought it was wonderful (apparently)

The Tetraps (an anagram of pet rats) and also a play on tetra meaning four (for their 4-way vision) was the merging of the two creatures the Bakers thought most horrible, bats and rats. McCoy's first scene with them was described by him as the most ridiculous thing he'd ever done – this from a man who spent part of his early career hammering nails up his nose. Nathan-Turner responded with, "You ain't seen nothing yet."

The pink sphere weapons however were some of the best effects Nathan-Turner had ever seen, although Morgan felt they were static and dull and felt he had been ill-advised. Morgan was new to effects work and felt he was bullied by the effects people into making decisions that affected the look of the show and felt it was one of the worst jobs he ever did.

The new season adapted the format that would see out the classic era series. Two four-parters and two three-parters. The three-parters had the same crew and director, but one was filmed only on location and one in the studio. Cartmel felt this was a masterstroke by Nathan-Turner, as it saved a lot of money

There's so much new stuff here. The theme is new too, welcome to Keff McCulloch's world. It's in the key of A minor and Nathan-Turner at the time felt it was the best ever (!!). Delia Derbyshire wasn't impressed, according to future who music curator Mark Ayers, mainly because the original these used radiophonic *music concrete*, but this is just played on a synthesiser. It also included the middle 8 in the opening titles, which was a first. McCulloch's music does get a lot of flak, but he should be praised for fitting in with the cartoonish nature of it all. One more thing before we head off away from music, this is the era of muzak and background tunes. Mainly popularised by *Eastenders* who always had pop songs in the back of their sets *Doctor Who* would do it too, but without paying royalties. It's a real hallmark of this era and rarely noted, so we have muzak here on Lakertya, rock n roll in later stories, muzak again in *The Happiness Patrol*, I could go on...

The titles were also new and went to a company called CAL video, who created the universe exploding theme. There was a new logo too, which caused all sorts of problems for Target and their novelizations. It's not used much now and is often described as 'crap one' in trendy books like these.

We're nearly done; the show was moved back to weekly slot, a 'wonderful move' according to Nathan Turner. He failed to mention it was in the graveyard slot, opposite *Coronation Street*.

The Bakers never wrote for *Doctor Who* again, although they assure us it was their decision.

Part 1*

Excerpts from the TARDIS dictionary disc: Regenerate *(verb): to assume a new physical form (of Time Lords, etc.)* Rani *(noun): a deadly adversary of the Doctor.* Lakertya *(noun): a planet inhabited by serpentine humanoids, until recently peaceful...* - RT (As usual these comments come from the Radio Times. Can you spot there's a new script editor?)

It won't do us any harm to give a little recap as to the circumstances that this was made. *Doctor Who,* the TV show had flown too close to the sun and its hubris had caused its downfall. The show had become a ghastly over-lit mess of continuity and nonsense. There was no mystery, no point to the show except that it got made every year and a dwindling number of people watched it, and a hard-core bunch of outcasts (including me) remained fanatical and perhaps a little over hysterical. Behind the scenes the show had effectively been cancelled but brought back at the last minute. The show's punishment was for it to be ignored by the bosses and placed in a time slot guaranteed to make it fail. The bosses were biding their time so they *can* cancel it properly having learned from the mistakes they trying to cancel it before. The Producer has had all his confidence sapped by the cancellation and has tried to move on. The old script editor has left in a fury when he really should have gone a year before. The actor playing the Doctor has been sacked and refused to do a regeneration scene. Oh, and Bonnie Langford is the companion. There are no scripts, no new ideas. This show is a car crash. But they have 14 episodes to make. You can imagine how bad it could be can't you...?

And the weird thing about *Time and the Rani* is that it hasn't got a hope in hell, but it's trying so hard. Sometimes age helps a story, sometimes the memory cheats, but here neither is true. The opening shots are a prologue (which is a first by the way) a bit like you would have at the start of a modern episode. The background music sounds like a vintage computer game. It's so amateurish, with the bleep noises, as we watch the badly animated computer animated star field. The TARDIS is zapped and then the paintbox computer kit comes out again to make a quarry get a pink sky. Mark Greenstreet, blond hunk *de jour* (who Nathan-Turner would have been *aware* of I'm sure) wearing green alien stuff watches the TARDIS arc across the pink sky and crash, sort of.

In the TARDIS the Doctor and Mel lie prone; in comes the Rani with a massive space gun and accompanied by a giant Muppet to say the immortal Pip and Jane line: "Leave the girl, it's the man I want." Camply brilliant, I don't deny. The hairy Muppet thing goes to the 6th Doctor's costume, the body turns and the face is obscured by light. He's regenerating!

Much has been made of the fact that the Sixth Doctor regenerates in such feeble circumstances, especially as Mel, a mere puny human doesn't seem to suffer any ill effects. Fear not, fandom of course has the answer. Gary Russell wrote a book for the BBC 'Past Doctors' range called *Spiral Scratch*, which explains it all. I wouldn't bother reading it, or even locating it, a second-hand copy is at least £10-£20 on eBay (I really need to get into my loft and start selling some of my stuff you know). Essentially, in *Spiral Scratch* the Doctor and Mel wander round lots of alternate universes, as some seem to be winking out of existence. In defeating the super being responsible the Doctor is fatally weakened. Then the Rani attacks. You see? Happy now? No? Well the Virgin Books range have other explanations. Essentially these seem to be that the 7th Doctor thought the 6th Doctor was a bit crap and forced the 6th into the Rani's trap to induce his regeneration, allowing the 7th Doctor to become Time's Champion. No? Oh, OK then, in 2015 Big Finish – of course - has an answer to what happened for about £40. You decide. Oh and while we're in continuity hell, there's no explanation of how the Rani escaped *her* last escapade – you remember with the Tyrannosaurus Rex?

Now the titles. Dear Lord, the theme is truly, truly horrible. Also, the key is wrong, losing all the mystery that the key of E minor gave it. As I've noted Delia Derbyshire hated this version. She was not alone. The titles are a mess of blue and pink and Nathan-Turner finally gets his way, getting the Doctor to wink in the titles.

It gets worse. You know a story is in trouble when in the first scene a green-skinned alien (Sarn) puts Albert Einstein to sleep in a pod. An older alien (a Lakertyan called Beyuz) oversees. The Rani seems to be in a foul mood:

"I find your incompetence more than enough without listening to your puerile opinions," she growls. Do Pip and Jane talk like that at home?

Then Sylvester's first scene is...excruciating. It involves a niceish little Doctory piece, then a poorly acted point at the Rani, a terrible exclamation of: "The Rani!" - and a pratfall. The Rani's: "this is idiotic" summed up the views of the few members of the public still watching. Genuinely awful. Fortunately McCoy will improve, then he overacts his, "I'll smash it pieces" line.

The Rani calls in Urak one of the hairy Muppets (tetrap), but we don't see its face. McCoy looks amused by the advancing Muppet and bemused when he is covered by the tetrap's net weapon. The Rani injects the Doctor with something to make him get amnesia.

Back at the TARDIS Mark Greenstreet a Lakertyan picks up Mel. She escapes, bumps into another Lakertyan, who is killed in a sort of electronic bubble mine. Here's the thing: Langford's running is the most convincing running we've seen from a companion in ages. I'm trying here! In addition, apart for the over reliance on pink the bubble trap effect is absolutely brilliant. Probably the best we've seen in the series to this point. The Lakertyan is sort of bounced around and explodes in the side of a cliff. I really hate to say it, but it's awesome.

Then we get the next stupid thing in this episode. The Rani pretending to be Mel to fool the Doctor. I mean how does she even know his companion's name *is* Mel, and can replicate her wardrobe? And hair? Yes, yes Kate O'Mara is better at playing Mel than Bonnie Langford, and some could argue it's a bit cruel of the show to expose Langford in this way.

The Doctor gives us his first malapropism. 'Bull in a barber shop,' followed by 'fit as a trombone'. The Rani is trying the con the Doctor into fixing her machine, because he's an expert in thermodynamics. Is he, or did Pip and Jane just think it sounded good? Oh, and now he's playing the spoons. 'A bad workman blames his fools.'

The Lakertyans and Mel do typical 1980s *Doctor Who* running. The Lakertyans runs without moving his arms – that illustrates they're alien, you see. In the TARDIS the Doctor gives us a costume scene. He dresses as Napoleon, then sort of Tom Baker, sort of Pertwee, sort of Davison and terrible jokes. Then he finds his own question mark outfit. 'Absence makes the nose grow longer,' says the Doctor. Come on let's see the tetraps, stop teasing. They look a bit cuddly. Mel gets caught in a bubble trap and screams to the credits.

Part 2 *

Excerpts from the TARDIS dictionary disc: Doctor *(noun): a traveller in time and space.* Amnesiac *(adjective): in a state of loss of memory.* Catspaw *(noun): person manipulated for unknown reasons – RT*

Of course the previous episode was virtually unwatchable from a production perspective and it carries on with the cliff-hanger resolve being Mel getting lucky and landing in water. A few minutes later we get our first proper look at the tetraps. Pretty impressive, although with rather pointless eyes on each side of their head, Mel gives us a good scream as she sees it. Her Lakertyan friend sprays it with something.

The Doctor is helping the Rani/Mel with her machines. He says he made a mistake and 'the heat radiation from the catalyst was of the wrong frequency'. Hmmm wrong in so many ways. The Doctor seems to work out that the Rani is not Mel because 'Mel' has forgotten what C.P Snow had to say about thermodynamics. Now this opens up another minefield, as C.P Snow tended to talk about the gulf between scientists and other intellectuals, not thermodynamics itself. He did mention thermodynamics in *The Two Cultures and the Scientific Revolution*. It's weird that the Doctor, an 'expert' in thermodynamics uses C.P Snow full stop. It's like being an expert in television production and using the audience of a TV show as your reference point for how to produce a TV show. Unless the Doctor meant Snow's pithy summing up of the laws of thermodynamics: 'You can't win. You can't break even. You can't quit the game.' And you'd think the Rani would know this, as she has got Einstein captured over there, and she must have captured him for a reason.

"Would PHB or PES be useful for the machine?" asks the Rani/Mel.

What a dumb question! Polyhydroxybutrate and Polyethersulphone are both polymers that Pip and Jane looked up in their big book of 'facts we use to show we do our research.' That's the only reason the line is in. The two polymers are very different. The Doctor goes for PHB, as it's biodegradable: More of the Baker's limited research. The Rani thinks the Lakertyans may have some PES: the PHB is unviable because there's no sugar or starch on Lakertya. Hello! She goes to get some, but the tetraps get her by mistake on her wild polymer chase.

Mark Greenstreet meets his mother Faroon, played by Wanda Bentham (Benedict Cumberbatch's mother). She tries to stop him being a rebel and to start being an appeaser. Bentham hated her costume, calling her character Faroon the balloon.

The Doctor and Mel meet and the scene is nearly good, just acted badly. McCoy is less good at the Bakers' dialogue than Colin Baker was. It doesn't suit him at all. After a few arguments. Mel and the Doctor decide they

36

are each other and the Doctor gives us the lowdown on strange matter (found in an asteroid that could destroy 'this corner of the Galaxy'), and reveals his age to be 953 – the combination lock to the geniuses. The Rani's geniuses are all from Earth, except the Doctor. Bit hard to fathom. Hang on: Louis Pasteur, was a genius? He was good but hardly able to manipulate the universe! Besides, the Rani probably knows more than him. The Doctor gets surrounded by tetraps as the Rani gives up her disguise.

Part 3 *

Excerpts from the TARDIS dictionary disc: Plasma *(noun): substance found in human blood.* Tetraps *(noun): savage extra-terrestrial with strange dietary habits.* Eyrie *(noun): dwelling place for large winged creatures with one entrance and no exit – RT*

In the tetraps' bat lair McCoy's does more jokey stuff. The comedy will die down, but the fact that he can't go round a corner without having a laugh is a shame. The tetraps hanging from the ceiling is a great shot by the way. He's saved by some more food being served up. The tetraps speak like everyone else in Pip and Jane world. More pratfalls with a thermistor and an umbrella.

Mel gets caught by more tetraps and even Mel finds that her scream threshold is reached, as she can barely do her second one and it comes out as an 'aaaaaah'. The Doctor pushes one into a trap with barely a thought, having just proclaimed his non-violent attitude in the previous scene. The Rani keeps the leader of the Lakertyans at bay by threatening them with insects. Not really seen on screen. Mel is hanging upside down in the tetrap cave and the Doctor is fooled by a hologram of Mel. Behind the door of the Rani's lab is a giant brain...that expands and throbs. The Doctor is captured and the geniuses are being used to make the brain cleverer. A goodish cliff-hanger.

Part 4 *

Excerpts from the TARDIS dictionary disc: Catalyst *(noun) vital substance that allows change of events to proceed.* Countdown *(noun): announcement of the last remaining seconds before something takes place.* Armageddon *(noun): the end of the world – RT*

The tetraps are just stupid. I mean they spout Bakeresque dialogue and are baddies, but why precisely do they need to be in costume? They don't do anything much except be monsters because *Doctor Who* 'has monsters in.' The Doctor adds ludicrousness to the brain's intelligence. The Rani goes on about Helium-2 fusion, creating chronons and creating a time manipulator. The Doctor worries about Mrs Malaprop not being created, which is nearly a good line. The Rani

38

is going to manipulate evolution. The giant brain creates loyhargil (Holy Grail) the lightweight substitute for strange matter that will make it all work. Mel, a computer expert from 1986 is able to defuse booby traps on Lakertya. There's a big countdown. The music during these sequences, which has been annoyingly intrusive and cloyingly pan pipe suddenly goes for the *Doctor Who* theme tune played on a crap computer. It's...diabolical.

The Rani blows everything up and the rocket heads for space but misses the asteroid. The Rani doesn't hang about and leaves. Why does the Rani's TARDIS, not blend in with the surroundings? It's a pyramid. The Doctor takes the geniuses back.

Verdict:

Let's get some positives (or if you prefer, some non-negatives) out the way first. John Nathan-Turner described making the whole of Season 24 as 'running on the spot' and no more is this obvious than here. It was commissioned in rush, it doesn't help that the design has dated horribly, but it has to be said that Langford gives her best performance, but that's not saying much. The Bakers sort of keep their dialogue in-check, but the science and plot remain childish at best, and although McCoy's cartoon portrayal here is poor by other actors' standards, he is the Doctor. I have forgotten Colin Baker. . McCoy, when he re-watched it felt it wasn't as bad as it was portrayed, but concedes that as it was written for Colin Baker - it was like a coat that doesn't quite fit. And this is clutching at straws but I suppose the beauty of low points is that the only way is up, or as Winston Churchill would have it: 'when you're in he'll keep going.'

No, no I can't do it. Let's look at some other people's comments: Lance Parkin called it the most 'relentlessly uninspired story in all of *Doctor Who.*' Apparently Cartmel's agent saw the first episode, rang him and exclaimed, 'I thought you were one of the good guys!' Kim Newman, in his brilliant book on *Doctor Who* for the BFI writes: "McCoy had the misfortune to be cast when the series had run low on inspiration, shucking off so many identities and formats that it could only cobble together scraps and limp through seasons."

Look, there's no getting around the fact that Part 1 really is as bad as *Doctor Who* ever gets; McCoy is excruciating. The remaining three parts aren't so bad, but the nasty taste lingers. I re-watched this on November 24th. 2013. Yes, the day after *The Day of the Doctor* was first screened, one day after the most orgiastic day of *Doctor Who*ness ever. Unfair I know, but how can this lack so much of what now makes *Doctor Who* what it is. When modern documentaries are made about *Doctor Who* they often reduce the McCoy era to a footnote, as do most of the reference books. This story is never going to help the case.

So, despite The Art of Noise-style synth bursts (look them up) this is awful. Avoid. And it's so bad I've forgotten it's a regeneration story. It's worse than *The Twin Dilemma* though, and what makes it hard to swallow (and yes this is directed at all the apologists for Season 24 out there) is that if, like me you've watched it all in order, episode-by-episode there is a direct link to the past. This might be OK as a late night post-pub giggle fest, but when placed in order and in context with the show's past, it's embarrassing. The very first episode of *Doctor Who* is one of the greatest pieces of television ever produced. The original music has been called the greatest piece of British electronic music (Bob Stanley) and now we have this ghastly parody of both. It's hard to believe anyone could have let this happen

One final positive then: if you swap *Remembrance of the Daleks* around with *Battlefield* then there is a case for saying each McCoy story is better than the last...it's uphill all the way from now on then!

Other famous reviews: "It may be childish at times but there's a real sense of energy in the storytelling and it's got some fabulous special effects (7/10)"- Doctor Who The Episode Guide by Mark Campbell (Pocket Essentials) – as is traditional at this time I should note that the author of this book rated Jon Pertwee's Spearhead from Space at 4/10, so please bear that in mind when reading the comments.

"Feels like the watered-down dregs of the Colin Baker era" – Who's Next – an unofficial and unauthorised guide to Doctor Who (Clapham, Robson, Smith – Virgin).

"If it was truncated into three episodes, and came with a self-lobotomising kit, this might have been a passable adventure romp. But it isn't" – Doctor Who – The Discontinuity Guide (Topping, Day, Cornell – Virgin).

Ratings: 4.63 million (81st in the ranking for the week) (182 rated Doctor Who story in terms of chart placing).

Position in DWM top 200: 198th (still over-rated!). 239th out of 241 in 2013 DWM poll, still the third worst story ever!

What have we discovered? The show should have been left to die.

Paradise Towers

One Line Summary: The 'Cartmel Masterplan' starts by the ripping off a different style of science fiction to that previously plagiarised by *Doctor Who*.

Written by: Stephen Wyatt - A Cambridge university graduate and Footlights player, just like Douglas Adams. He worked in education and community theatre but eventually drifted towards freelance writing. His first piece of commissioned work was a play called *Claws* (see below). Went on to follow Cartmel to write for hospital soap *Casualty*.

Directed by: Nick Mallett - Started off as a dancer but joined the BBC as a studio manager in radio, then a floor manager in TV. He completed the BBC's director's course and worked on training films, *Crossroads* and *Spitting Image*. He directed the first four episodes of *The Trial of a Time Lord*.

Anything else before we start?

Once the nightmare of *Time and Rani* was out of the way Cartmel could start to develop his own ideas. He already had a reading list, essentially Alan Moore's comic work, including *Halo Jones*. More bizarrely it also included the academic tome *Doctor Who –The Unfolding Text*, which was lying around the office – yes I've discussed this book before (see Volumes 4 and 5). All he needed now was writers...

According to Cartmel, Wyatt sought out Cartmel to write for the show, although Nathan-Turner contradicts this. Wyatt confirms the Nathan-Turner version. Wyatt worked in the BBC script department and rang up various producers looking for work. When he called Nathan-Turner he was put in contact with Cartmel. It was only the second script Wyatt had written for television. The first, *Claws*, a comedy had also just been on BBC1. He enjoyed the freedom *Doctor Who* gave him. He had just finished reading J G Ballard's *High Rise* and mentioned it to Cartmel. They went to the pub and the idea grew. Then, they met with Nathan-Turner and he was happy to go for it. It was the first script Cartmel commissioned.

Written in 1975, *High Rise* was set in a tower block where things go wrong and the residents form gangs. To say *Paradise Towers* is a play on it is an understatement, although the reason the residents stay in the block in the *Doctor Who* version is less clear. Wyatt now plays down the *High Rise* influence – well you would - and claims that visiting friends who lived in tower blocks in the East End was also a source. He noted how you'd get out a lift and there'd be no indication in the lift as to what floor you had arrived on. Local youths leapt in and pressed all the buttons, so you could be getting out anywhere.

Cartmel loved the first draft and loved the stage directions: like, 'he smiled like only a zombie can'. Cartmel suggested the girl gangs and the colours, which Cartmel hoped anticipated LA Gang culture - it didn't. He also praised Wyatt's thoughtful use of slang, this despite not knowing who was going to be cast as the Doctor.

Nathan-Turner was delighted with the quality of the cast, which included Richard Briers as the Chief Caretaker. Briers didn't think much of appearing in *Doctor Who* and enjoyed the opportunity to over-act. He claims Mallet chose him because he was a funny man, which raises questions about the tonal direction of the piece. Wyatt puts a different slant on this because he claims he recommended T P McKenna (Captain Cook in *The Greatest Show in the Galaxy)* to play the role, but Nathan-Turner turned him down, wanting a bigger name. So who did cast Briers?

Briers claims Nathan-Turner was worried about him going over the top (see *Timelash* in Volume 6 for why) and this encouraged Briers even more. "(John Nathan-Turner) was looking at me in a funny old-fashioned way, we were rehearsing it, and I thought this guy I was playing wanted to rule the world and is completely mad. So that's the way I was playing it. And he (Nathan-Turner) was looking at me and looking at me, and I thought, 'He doesn't seem to like me very much'. In the end the director, who'd had a chat with him, came to me and said, 'He's very worried about you', I said, 'I know, I got the vibes. What's wrong?' and he said, 'He thinks you're over-playing it'. I said, 'Oh, I thought it was that kind of a part. I don't see how you can underplay Adolf Hitler, if you want to rule the world you can't be very subtle about it'. He said, 'No, he's very worried about it'. But my sidekick (Clive Merrison) said, 'Never mind what he says, you do it your way, it's very funny' and I said, 'Okay' and in fact you know I think I nearly lost the job. I think he thought I was sending it up, but I was just simply over-acting."

Cartmel wasn't impressed with the over-acting either but couldn't decide if it was Briers or Mallet who was to blame. Casting seemed a problem throughout; the guards should have been fat and overweight, but the casting director didn't do that, and Pex, well he should have been a giant muscle man. Cartmel felt this was a 'screw up.'

"Stephen (Wyatt's) gag - which I wholeheartedly endorsed - was the idea that this guy was a total muscle man who fucks things up because he's incredibly stupid. He ends up being a victim. But when they cast it, they got Howard Cooke, who was cast by Nick Mallet. Nick didn't have the same vision for Pex, he was just concerned with getting a good actor who could do the business. So (Wyatt) was disappointed with that. It was a joke that was screwed up by the casting, but at least we ended up with a good actor."

Langford's main memory was of the freezing swimming pool, which she mentions in all of her interviews about the show. The robots came in for criticism and their lack of menace – even by the cast, but there was a feeling that it needed to be light to distract from the very dark themes here.

Cartmel explains: "It's time for me to make another speech here. We started with certain elements. It's set in a high rise that became a decaying urban maze. There's the hierarchy of the people who manage the building, and the fascistic girl gang (just to please me). But we needed a monster. And we went to see John and said, What about tentacles? They could come out through the ventilation grilles. And he said, 'Tentacles are difficult', spoken with the knowing manner of a man who's tried tentacles before."

"John knew the constraints of the BBC budget, and he knew what you could do with the BBC effects department. What you're really talking about is working on a limited budget and in a limited time span. The script said a killer robot drags a girl off and what you get is what you've just described. If it had been shot like a James Cameron film, you'd be reminiscing about how incredibly scary those things were. Would that we'd had those sort of budgets, or the sort of gifted design you get in *Terminator* which was a relatively low budget movie. McCoy was still a bit nervous about playing the role but Mallet recalls he was more malleable than Baker. Baker would never improvise: McCoy was made for it.

Part 1 *** (for the novelty) * (for the execution)

Paradise Towers won a lot of awards back in the 21ˢᵗ century. It might even be a nice place to live now, if it weren't for the Kangs, the Caretakers and the strange behaviour of the Mark 7 Megapodic Cleaners – RT

The theme music is like an annoying bee buzzing out of tune and the background music is still dire. We see graffiti and 1980s kids when we should see the future. The Doctor and Mel are at Paradise Towers and Mel is excited about the pool. Err, isn't there one in the TARDIS? Phew, a reference to it, it's leaky. Paradise Towers is one of the great architectural achievements of the 21st century but is now a graffitied litter- strewn mess, with rats and Banksie style graffiti.

We meet the caretakers, who have bureaucratic names and Richard Briers is doing his comedy adenoidal voice. Their uniforms are a bit stylised too but they're essentially Nazis. The Doctor and Mel meet the red Kangs, who scream and chant and say things like 'cowardly cutlets'. One is called 'Bin Liner' and another 'Fire Escape'. This seemed weird at the time but now we know it's very Stephen Wyatt. The greeting 'haka' is a nice scene ruined by the stupid music. Dudley Simpson might have made it watchable. The last yellow Kang is dead and found in the back of some cleaning machines. There are no boys in Paradise Towers. They're fighting a war. The cleaning machines are killing people, but there is no tension.

The Doctor and Mel get split up, the Doctor caught by the caretakers and Mel has tea and cake with two old ladies: Tilda and Tabby. Pex bursts into the room. He protects the towers and he looks a right wuss. Bad casting. The Doctor runs from a very slow cleaning machine.

The Doctor meets the Chief Caretaker who hails him as the Chief Architect then decides he should be killed, as the episode needs to end.

Part 2 -1*

It's an average day in Paradise Towers. The Rezzies have their door kicked in, the Kangs are reloading their crossbows and the Caretakers are dying in the corridors – RT

This is such a bleak world, such a bleak idea but it's so weirdly played. It's also hugely different, which makes it refreshing at best. Having said that this is probably my least favourite episode of *Doctor Who* ever: the very epitome of what the show isn't.

Richard Briers is the problem: one of the great TV actors of his generation he's having enormous fun in his exaggerated costume and Hitler moustache. And it's the final nail in the believability coffin. The vision of this piece has been totally missed.

The Doctor is to be killed despite his protestations that he is not the Great Architect. Pex bends iron bars and the Doctor tries to have a philosophical conversation with his caretaker guards as the incidental music tries to put you off what is quite a good scene by being totally incongruous. Pity the scene ends with the Doctor's escape being more ludicrous than the music (hard to imagine). Utterly unrealistic and worthy of the Chuckle Brothers.

The idea of a war where the young men went fight and never came back is good, but undermined by the casting decisions to cast youngish men as caretakers and as for the madness of Pex's casting...and what's annoying is that with the sound down there could be moments of macabre brilliance. Take the next scene with Tilda and Tabby who are clearly eating something gruesome followed by an almost good shot of the cleaning robot catching up with the Doctor. The scene is ruined by the music then ruined by the choice of shots and then ruined by McCoy being unable to fall without making it funny. But we do get a scene that I bet was lovely on paper as the Doctor gets the red Kangs lemonade from a vending machine. If it had been any Doctor bar McCoy, Davison or Colin the scene would have been charming, but in 1980s *Who*, it just is.

The Chief Caretaker is feeding a pair of neon eyes that says 'hungry' a lot and Pex hid from the war. And then I realise something. Langford's stagy acting fits with the music. It's the only thing that gels, but it ain't *Doctor Who*. The Doctor and the red Kangs are attacked by the caretakers, another Doctorish speech drowned by synths and Mel is about to be murdered by Tilda and Tabby. Where do the Kangs get their hair dye from?

Part 3 **

In which the Doctor gets his second chance at the 327 appendix 3 subsection 9 death and Mel finds out whether the muscle brain really is a scaredy cat - RT

We ought to look at the subtexts here. These often crop up in studio-bound stories, because they don't look real. Here we have an allegorical look at the classical Stanford prison experiment, where the caretakers become prison officers just because they have the uniform.

And it took three parts for us to see a shot of Paradise Towers. It's a drawing of a tower block. It poses more questions than answers. One longs for dear Robert Holmes to give a character one throwaway line to paint the world. In fact this could be a Holmes idea, but badly done of course.

and Tabby die by means of metal claw from the waste disposal; the thing in the basement is hungry. Pex does nothing. It's nearly a good scene but do I need to spell out why it doesn't work? Mel goes for the swimming pool and Briers and McCoy go head to head.

And, at last McCoy gets it, as he plays his role beautifully against Briers' caricature. Not once does he do anything silly.

Why is the Doctor walking round with an umbrella? Mercifully not the question mark one. Mel gets to the basement the chief gets sent there too and the Doctor works out that Kroagnon, the Great Architect was a nutter and probably buried down there. Mel gets to the pool, not a very impressive pool. A cleaning robot goes for them, the Chief is killed and the Doctor is throttled by a cleaning machine.

Part 4 *

No ball games. No flyposts. No escape – RT

The Doctor is rescued by having a crap crossbow fired at the robot. Richard Briers is possessed silver-faced and really taking the opportunity to overact. The Doctor describes Kroagnon taking over the Chief Caretaker's body as corpoelectroscopy, which is entirely made-up and nonsense. I know my hypocrisy at hating Pip and Jane's well-researched nonsense means I should embrace Wyatt's made-up nonsense but I don't, so there. Remarkably the 'Mel gets attacked by the pool cleaner' scene is very good and well shot, though Pex's pathetic behaviour is getting annoying. Everyone gets together to fight Kroagnon, even Pex has a role. It's quite nice.

52

Pex takes out the Architect, sacrificing himself, but it's all rather childish. Everyone lives happily ever after.

One thing we must say in its favour is that of course this is the first story since *Vengeance on Varos* that has no previous references to *Doctor Who* lore. And for that we should be grateful.

Verdict:

As noted before under *Terminus* and *Warriors' Gate* hard science fiction doesn't really work on *Doctor Who*, so throwing this pure science fiction idea at our show really doesn't work, although it might just have done if they had cast it better and scored it better. Although this will never be anybody's favourite story, it is utterly different from what has gone before in story type and...well, to the watching viewer at the time it was either a new beginning or the beginning of the end. Actually it was both.

Its other big crime is a lack of context, which contributes to the childish feel. Where is this tower? Why don't the residents leave? What war? Why keep the Great Architect secret? Why not foreshadow his weirdness at the start and allow our knowledge to make it creepier? If they had done that then the weirdness of Part 1 could have been avoided. A darker, dirtier, well-cast, well-made, well-sound tracked, well-contextualised version of this might have been an all-time classic, it's not too far removed from *The Sunmakers* if you think about it.

Gareth Roberts, in his usual style, claims that by 1986 *Doctor Who* whiffed like the carpet in a comic shop, with so many continuity references. He feels Season 24 is like opening the window, switching on the air con and squirting lemon disinfectant around with abandon. He then asserts that this feels more like *Doctor Who* than anything since *The Horns of Nimon*. Don't you love diverse opinion?

Other famous reviews: "The script is a cross between Alan Bennett and Ackbourne (sic) while Briers is hilarious as the Hitleresque chief caretaker. The story's strength lies in its expert balancing of humour and horror (9/10)" – Episode Guide (that's higher than *Genesis of Daleks* folks!).

"Very peculiar in terms of style, tone and content but rather ordinary in terms of quality" - Who's Next.

"A lovely basic idea, somewhat thwarted by its uncertain tone and presentation. The caretakers look like rejects from the Village People, and when they say 'All hail the Great Architect' they have their hands under their noses in clear tribute to Basil Fawlty. There is a degree of semantic cleverness ('taken to the cleaners', 'brain quarters', 'cowardly cutlet', etc.), and much mockery of the rule bound caretakers, but it just doesn't quite work." – Discontinuity Guide.

Ratings: 4.93 million 86th (194)

Position in DWM top 200: 193rd, 230th in 2013
What have we discovered? That Stephen Wyatt might be good, if the rest of the team can raise their game.

Delta and the Bannermen

One Line Summary: *Hi de Hi* meets *Doctor Who*

Written by: Malcolm Kohll: Born in Southern Africa, he trained as journalist and came to London to do postgraduate work in film and television. He found it hard to break into script writing for films and this was one his first paid commissions. After he did *Who*, he wrote *The Fourth Reich*, a African set political thriller thing for South African television. He's now head of Film at the South African Film School (AFDA).

Directed by: Chris Clough: from Yorkshire. He had trained as an accountant but gave it up to read English Literature at university. He had come to directing via Granada TV, where he worked as researcher. He got some work directing on soap operas like *Brookside* and *Eastenders*, which is where Nathan-Turner saw his work. He directed the last two stories of the Colin Baker era, which were quite well received at the time.

Anything else before we start?

Kohll was an old pal of Cartmel, who described him as a thriller writer. Nathan-Turner wanted to get away from the Home Counties and suggested Wales. Kohll set it in a holiday camp in Wales because he had been on holiday to Barry Island, where the story was filmed.

Actually he claims he drove past the dilapidated Butlin's site and thought, 'what a shame,' and 'how wonderful, the hopes and dreams of working class people'. He also thought – 'what a location!'

Again, the late re-commission by the BBC meant this was written in a rush. Nathan-Turner suggested the 1950s setting in discussions about a 20th Century setting that wasn't the 1960s. Kohll had been watching balletic King Hu movies, with their faceless banner-carrying armies and liked their look. He's also been learning about bees.... He wrote the Vincent motorbike into the story because he was a fan and wanted to sit on one.

The initial script for Part 1 was declared 'good' although it was requested that the battle scene be moved to a slate quarry. "It wouldn't be Doctor Who without it," quipped Kohll. Nathan-Turner however felt that Part 2 was the worst script he'd ever seen. It was like a lukewarm sitcom. A 48-hour weekend session with Cartmel sorted it out. Despite the changes Nathan-Turner felt it was as close as *Doctor Who* came to a musical, and he said it pretending he wasn't appalled by the idea (I'm sure Nathan-Turner loved a good musical). They saved money by getting Keff McCulloch to recreate the songs of the 1950s rather than pay royalties for the original recordings. The story was set in 1959 to give more song choice. Kohll had input in which songs were chosen, which delighted him.

Although Cartmel felt this wasn't the best script he acknowledges it was the one the cast and crew got most excited about. Clough felt it was his favourite because of the nostalgia. Kohll was impressed by the casting, especially veteran stand-up comedian Ken Dodd, who surprised him.

Yes Ken Dodd - the part was originally offered to Bob Monkhouse (another stand-up comedian), who has a better acting track record, but he couldn't do it because a health scare. Clough cast him: "Was Ken Dodd controversial?" asks Clough. "It worked – it was my idea. It's a small part, but it's a fun cameo. I liked the idea of this build-up – the Doctor and Mel arriving at a Toll port that only has its landing light on, and you then get the tension of 'What's lurking there?', and instead of something nasty, you get Doddy coming out with his razzer going 'Hello, welcome! Surprise, surprise! You've won a prize!'"

McCoy wished he'd been brave enough to give Dodd direction on how to play his death scene, which was very over the top. The scene was filmed at 3 a.m. in an aerodrome near the Barry Island holiday camp.

The title of the story is very much like rock 'n' roll bands of the time but also plays off Echo and the Bunnymen, who were big at the time, although Echo was the drum machine in that band.

The original choice for the female lead Ray injured herself learning to pride the scooter she claimed she could ride when she auditioned so the part went to Sara Griffiths. She was mooted as a possible companion (Mel's days were numbered) in the end that would be

58

for the next young female role in the next story. Cartmel says: "We wrote two stories, each with a potential companion in mind, so John could get them on, shoot their shows and decide from there. If he'd chosen Sara Griffiths, we could have done great stuff with her too. I'm terribly fond of Sophie Aldred, so I'm glad we chose her, but the qualities she had in common with Sara Griffiths were being spunkier than Mel." Sara Griffiths couldn't ride the scooter either; there's a good out-take of her failing to ride the bike.

At rehearsals veteran actor Stubby Kaye said 'Hot damn! He stood up to that big bugger didn't he!" on hearing the Doctor Gavrok denouncement scene. Bless!

Cartmel remembers two other things about the shoot. "I remember we turned up - in a quarry - to do those opening sequences of Delta fleeing her planet and she had the natives of the planet with her. And the people who were responsible for making the aliens look alien, what they'd done was stuck some cotton wool on their faces and dyed it green. We are all working to the limits of our professionalism. Then me, John and the director turn up and you've got the aliens running around with cotton wool stuck to their faces. "And none of this is planned, nobody wants this to happen. I remember when we were doing the press screening at BAFTA and I was sitting next to this woman journalist and she saw this guy's face and she snorted with derisive laughter. When we turned up for that day on location and saw those aliens, we were so enraged. Everyone had tried so hard, to the best of their abilities but somebody else had thought well, we can just get away with something. And then that journalist's response, people just can't take it seriously after seeing that. Someone just didn't try."

Part 1 ****

It's destination Disneyland and the year is 1959. The Doctor and Mel are expecting rock'n'roll, beehive hairdos, 'sputniks' and possibly Mickey Mouse. What they're going to get is Delta and the Bannermen – RT

Let's not beat around the bush, the opening battle scene with the lovely paintboxed planet in the background is as good we've ever seen. And it seems they've found a guest star who's playing it straight too (Don Henderson as Gavrok) and only the music annoys. Oh, and the question mark umbrella, which makes its debut here. It was McCoy's idea. Irrespective of the minor quibbles this is already better than the previous eight horrible episodes. Even the ship taking off is great as the titular Delta (a Chimeron) escapes from the Bannermen's grasp. Clough nicked the flags on the backs of the Bannermen idea from Kurasawa. Steal from the best!

Look, I'm even going to give Ken Dodd a break, as the scene at the toll station looks brilliant. Ok Dodd is a bit annoying but the Doctor winning a competition is cool. The prize is a trip to Disneyland with some Navarino tourists and despite the Navarino costumes being hilariously bad, the idea is just lovely, so let's run with it, OK. Delta arrives and escapes on the Navarino rock 'n' roll coach/spacecraft too and Gavrok, the lead Bannerman, who misses Delta by a whisker culls Ken Dodd. This is really good, although the bus crashing into the 'satellite that's a bit like Sputnik' isn't great *and* bad science.

The bus is diverted by the prang and crash lands in a working holiday camp in Wales rather than Disneyland, with the satellite stuck in The grill of the coach - only in *Doctor Who*. If it's a 'working' holiday camp it doesn't explain the almost knee-high grass at the place.

Then Stubby Kaye driving a Morris Minor fools us with a real police box and uses the phone. His jacket is all wrong though for an American of that age and era. And, OK, why is a London police box in a Welsh field anyway? Kaye's mate seems to continue the long tradition of bad American accents in *Doctor Who* (see *The Gunfighters, Tomb of the Cybermen* for a start), well that is until you realise actor Morgan Deare is actually American, oops.

The Doctor meets a variety of characters including Ray (the non-Ace of this story), Billy the mechanic and the coach driver who proves to be an idiot. The party have to stay for 24 hours. And sadly the holiday camp scenes are so cheesy it takes away something from this pretty classy episode. It's all Sylvester McCoy smiling, as boys give him apples and a rock 'n' roll band who have Jeff McCulloch with a pony rail and a keyboard player. I mean, it's 1959, it's wrong!! And Ray, she's so annoying! Ray has been in love with Billy since they were kids but Billy doesn't have a Welsh accent. Hmmm. The memory has cheated here, I remember Ray fondly but dear me she's played with the stiltedness of someone who isn't used to being in front of a camera.

That bloke from the Flying Pickets playing Keillor (Garrison?) grasses up Delta to Gavrok in a broad Birmingham accent. The pod Delta has brought with her spouts a brilliantly horrible green baby alien and Keillor (named only in the credits) knows of the Doctor and plans to kill him too.

Part 2 ***

It's 1959. Mel's just discovered something very interesting about the life cycle of her new friend and the Doctor has been cornered by an alien bounty hunter wearing blue suede shoes –RT.

Good heavens, a decent resolve, as Keillor gets it from Gavrok remotely leaving his shoes behind, which is a bit cheesy, but you can't have it all. Billy, who has the hots for Delta, goes round to her chalet and sees the green alien baby. He takes it very well and completely blows this away as a serious story. I mean come on. Delta starts to tell him her story…

…we cut to the next morning and we see Hugh Lloyd playing a beekeeper being all Time Lordy and then we cut back to Delta finishing her story. I make that at least eight hours. How long *is* Delta's back-story? I mean she's only a typically spacey space girl for heaven's sake and as the story ends with "and now all my people are dead…" Well blimey I think even someone whose led an interesting life could cut it down to less than 8 hours.

The Doctor cuts out explanation time by showing the camp leader inside the TARDIS. I'm very uncomfortable about this, but it's a very modern thing to do. The Bannermen land rather well as the Americans watch. They don't kill the Americans, the music remains excruciating. Don Henderson remains the thing that anchors this. Brilliantly dark, as he kills all the bus passengers. The Chimerons are finished he yells and the Bannermen stick their tongues out rather amateurishly. But then Gavrok eating raw meat scene is awesome again, pity the music just doesn't hit the right tone. Then McCoy gets in on the act muscling up to Gavrok under a flag of truce. It…nearly works but the tone is woefully wrong. The Bannermen raise their weapons.

Part 3 **

The Doctor and Melanie (sic) are on holiday in the 1950s. The guitars are red, the suede shoes are blue and the Bannermen Warfleet is out for blood – RT.

A very weird non-resolve.

Keff McCulloch should be shot for his uncanny ability to screw up any scene with his music. On screen we get various driving around scenes and weird royal jelly allusions. And the Doctor has an uncanny ability to wear glasses in long shots in the bike. Various honey and booby trap shenanigans occur and the bees attack the Bannermen. Billy has been eating Chimeron food to turn him into a Chimeron. No, no, no!

Gavrok gets it from his own booby trap after the Chimeron child screams through the Tannoy, beeswax in the ears keeps the goodies safe. Nice *Odyssey* link. Billy goes with Delta, a rather sudden decision to go, but there are no male Chimerons left and he is their last hope. It's one of the stupidest things we've ever seen in *Doctor Who*. I'm sure Billy the mechanic couldn't have afforded a 1959 Fender Stratocaster on his wages. Same with the bike he gives Ray.

The story ends nicely with Goronwy (Hugh Lloyd) staring at the sky knowingly. Lovely.

Verdict:

Andrew Cartmel says: "It's not one of my favourite stories, but that's because I think various elements were pitted against it." And although you feel this is a step in the right direction this is excruciating at times. It's a micro story about a generic baddy chasing a generic goodie with awful music, clowning and clichés abounding. There are some terrible performances and some very 'I'm in *Doctor Who* performances' too. Although it's unique, it's not unique in a good way. And it's a waste of Don Henderson too.

I must concede that part one is pretty good and Lance Parkin rightly points out at least it's trying to be different and isn't generic like many of the stories of the previous few years. In summary *Delta*'s got a lot going for it: the alien biology; the huge back-story of these two alien cultures at war that was quite complex and interesting so it's worth not dismissing it out of hand, but the Season 24ness of it all does for it in the end.

Other famous reviews:

"A confident summery musical comedy with violent overtones. It's hard not to admire its sheer cheek (8/10)" – Episode Guide. (Do I need to say it?)

"A lurch in the right direction" – Who's Next.

"Confident, slick, and hugely enjoyable from beginning to end, *Delta and the Bannermen* isn't grim, gritty or cynical, and is thus tremendously adult. It roars with new style. This is the first real hint of McCoy's Doctor" – Discontinuity Guide.

Ratings: 5.27 million. 68th (172)

Position in DWM top 200: 180th -217th in 2013

What have we discovered? That all is not lost.

Dragonfire

One Line Summary: This is what you get when you ask an ex-Film Studies student to write for *Doctor Who*.

New cast Ace: Sophie Aldred - Born in Blackheath South London she read drama at Manchester University. She then worked in fringe theatre and working men's clubs to get her Equity union card. She was in a production of *Fiddler on the Roof* when she got the call to audition for Ray in *Delta and the Bannermen*; she didn't get that but made enough of an impression to be offered Ace. This would be her first television work. It's fair to say that Cartmel might have been a little bit in love with Aldred, he wasn't the only one.

Written by: Ian Briggs - another man who Cartmel had met at the BBC writers' workshop, along with Kohll and Robin Mukherjee. Briggs studied drama at Manchester University and after that worked in the theatre on lighting and design, including on some jazz shows.

Directed by: Chris Clough

Anything else before we start?

Cartmel was close to getting his vision in place, despite the objections from his Producer. "I wanted to choose the writers, I wanted to change the character of the show. Create a sense of wonder. Make the Doctor and enigma. Fuck the explanatory lumber of my 20 years of predecessors." There was an almost militant attitude to the rest of the world, the fans, the BBC etc. The criticism from uber fans was galling. It annoyed McCoy too, especially the attacks on Nathan-Turner. It had the advantage of getting people to raise their game.

As Cartmel and Briggs knew each other from script writing courses they bashed out ideas, because believe me Cartmel was going to commission Briggs come what may, despite him being clueless about *Doctor Who* and sci-fi in general. One idea was for a property developer to take over the TARDIS, which sounds very Douglas Adams, but Nathan-Turner rightly said the kids wouldn't get it: he TARDIS is bigger on the inside, full stop, move on, tell another story. The next Briggs' original idea was for a 14-year old financial wizard with a sidekick called Mr Spewey, or Fatboy in other versions. It was rejected, not because the baddie wore Hawaiian shirts, although Cartmel didn't want to offend Nathan-Turner.

Cartmel and Briggs worked together to get the story we know as *Dragonfire*. Cartmel liked the idea of the monster holding the jewel, which is the key to a spaceship. Cartmel reckoned it was far and away the best script of the year. The notorious 'semiotic thickness' scene was inserted by Cartmel as a joke, having got the *Doctor Who- The Unfolding Text* off the shelf again. Briggs loved it. Iceworld was of course based on the Bejam

68

frozen food stores, now known as Iceland. Kane was called Hess until quite late until the Nazi prisoner Rudolph Hess was rumoured to be being given a release and the name was changed.

Cartmel wrote Langford's leaving scene after the original one proved a little dry. McCoy complained about the dryness, although Briggs argues that it was like that because it was originally written as one for bit-part character Razorback (who turned into Glitz), then Ace, which doesn't make much sense. McCoy wanted to use the audition scene he'd used with Langford so Clough asked Cartmel for it. Cartmel rewrote it quickly and claims it was written on a napkin in the BBC canteen, or the Red Crush bar, depending on the source. Langford had decided to leave to reinvent herself. Her professionalism never doubted by the crew but in terms of the show, Cartmel had been stuck with Mel as created by the previous team. He wanted a much darker, dirtier, funkier, nastier companion and that certainly wasn't Langford's forte at all. In his words: "I don't know if you read *Love and Rockets*, but we were going for that sort of sisters-are-doing-it-for-themselves kind of thing, which was not Bonnie. We wanted a post-*Alien* teenage girl - again, that probably says something about my psyche. That was something Stephen Wyatt said - the hallmark of Season 24 is 'tough young bitches.'

Cartmel also made a conscious decision not to use the companion as a weary routine story device, not just to ask questions; although some of that is necessary.

More importantly, he wanted to avoid the standard cliché where you separate the Doctor and companion early in the story. And it's true especially in later stories, the Doctor and Ace are inseparable. Again, in Cartmel's words, "the fact that Ace began to blossom as a strong three-dimensional character is down to the fact that she was written by superb writers."

So they were looking for a new companion. Ray in *Delta and the Bannermen*, or Ace in *Dragonfire*. Cartmel liked them both but Nathan-Turner kept his options open when choosing the new companion. Aldred had been up for both parts and got this one. As she read the audition speech she felt she knew the character. You'll hear it told that she based it on three girls she knew, but Aldred denies this and says it was just gut feeling. As Nathan-Turner said in 1993: "well it was a weird situation in a way, because at the end of that season there were two stories both of which featured a possible on-going character. There was a young girl in *Dragonfire* and a young girl in *Delta and the Bannermen*, and the script editor Andrew Cartmel and I couldn't decide which story should end the season, and consequently the casting of these two young girls involved my office in a very major way because whichever one went out last would possibly hold the key to staying on in the show as a companion. But I'm delighted that it was Ace. I certainly don't think that Sophie was right for the other part. I'm not saying she couldn't have played it, but I think she was much righter for Ace, and I think the

70

combination of Ace with Doctor Number seven, Sylvester worked really well."

Having said that Nathan-Turner and Aldred didn't hit it off. Aldred didn't like the picture quality on her publicity cards for example and asked for them to be changed. Nathan-Turner gave her the 'who do you think you are?' talk. Aldred had never been in a studio before and didn't know what a gallery was. Luckily for her she hit it off with McCoy straight away and he gave her great advice on acting. McCoy's famous line about 'learn the lines and not try not to bump into the monsters' comes from this era.

Irrespective of how the character was created and who gets the most credit (Aldred for her portrayal, or Briggs for his characterisation) compared to Mel she was so well thought out, with even the costume being given some thought and looking in *The Face* magazine for ideas. The badges were thought out too and the *Blue Peter* badge was Aldred's own. Aldred's unshaved armpits caused a problem in one scene, Cartmel thought they were sexy, but he was outvoted by the floor manager.

The bad cliff-hanger in Part 1 made sense in the script, but on screen it didn't. The director got the blame and accepts it was a 'cock up', McCoy saying they fell in love with the stunt and forgot what it was about. Andrew Marson, writer on *Doctor Who Magazine* at the time was in the studio that day and claimed in his book about Nathan Turner that he couldn't believe anyone hadn't noticed the problem with the shot –hmmm.

Better was the *Raiders of the Lost Ark* melting shot, which took ten minutes to melt in real time with a no red colours directive for blood.

On set there were numerous delays whilst Tony Selby, returning to play Glitz had his sideburns checked to see that they were the same as the previous season. Glitz wasn't in the original draft, a character very similar to Glitz called Swordfish was, so it took little adapting to bring back the character.

For a bit of publicity this was billed as the 150th story, but it isn't if you count *The Trial of a Time Lord* as one story which it is. You think this sort of thing is annoying, well wait until Steven Moffat takes over. He almost relishes in confusing fans. I mean is *The Girl who Died* and *The Woman who Lived* a two-parter?

Part 1 ****

The trading colony of Iceworld has a teenage waitress called Ace, a dodgy dealer named Glitz, legends of treasure, and rumours of a dragon and a proprietor with a body temperature of minus 193 Celsius (sic). The Doctor and Mel are in for a cool reception – RT

"Oh you lucky, lucky people. You are the chosen ones," says Kracauer the guard on Iceworld to a bunch of mercenaries. What's this: an effective costume? Nice pickelhauber. Kracauer is named after Siegfried Kracauer, film theorist. In 1960, he released *Theory of Film: The Redemption of Physical Reality*, which argued that realism is the most important function of cinema. Ironic that he's a character in *Dragonfire*, but never mind. It's a great opening sequence, with a rebel, nicely explained liquid nitrogen and a baddie that kills by cold. See lads, it's not hard to make *Doctor Who*.

Nice model of Iceworld on Svartos and good aliens masks in a sort of giant freezer cabinet shop. Oh, and Miss Kael is asked for over the Tannoy (another film studies reference to Pauline Kael a well-known US film critic). This is good! In a bar Glitz turns up (see Volume 6). The Doctor is reading *The Doctor's Dilemma* (George Bernard Shaw) a play about having to choose which TB patients should get a revolutionary new treatment. The Doctor finds it funny at one point, no idea why. I can't find any allusions – damn. Glitz is trying to pay with an Asteroid Express card. Oops, first misstep.

Glitz has been conning Kane, the boss of ice world and we get some lovely dialogue with some guards. Kane of course is named after the main character in *Citizen Kane*, the film the regularly tops the greatest film of all time lists.

The guards threaten to take Glitz's ship off him, the Nosferatu, which is the name of the notorious silent film version of Dracula by Fritz Lang, and in some aspects still the scariest. Actually it's a fancy word for vampire that Bram Stoker used, but you get the point. It's either that or Glitz has named his ship after a Greek word meaning 'disease bearing', or a confused woman in the 19th century who thought the word was Romanian for 'vampire'. It wasn't.

Ace shows up as a waitress and fills us in about a dragon. The bar manager is called Anderson (after Lindsay Anderson leading light of the free cinema movement and the British new wave of filmmaking. He made *If...*). This character was renamed Eisenstein in the novel (I mean, for heaven's sake). Ace is not annoying. There's also treasure. Glitz is interested in the treasure too, and we get a 'real McCoy' joke. My sides are splitting – it was a rehearsal room adlib – the scripted line was 'the real oyster.'

Belazs the female guard wants Glitz's ship for herself but Kane shows her who's boss. Belazs is named after Bela Belazs Hungarian film critic, poet and aesthete. We really are some way from Terry Nation aren't we? Oh, and another guard is called McLuhan (Canadian philosopher of communication theory and a public intellectual. His work is viewed as one of the cornerstones of the study of media theory, as well as having practical applications in the advertising and television industries.) We also have Bazin (Andre another guard French film critic and theorist.) Talk about the weird contrast between the slapstick childish stuff alongside the smart arse stuff.

Meanwhile, to counter the Film Studies wackiness Ace pours a milkshake over an annoying woman customer and gets fired. Ace gives us some lovely, if unlikely back-story, which will only become relevant in Season 26 (except they didn't have a clue really). As we see it, it's just another childish aspect to this childish, but enjoyable tale. We also see Ace's love of homemade explosive nitro nine and chemistry. Of course Aldred is a breath of fresh air, although her street dialogue is bit over played here – she'll calm down.

I must also point out the *Wizard of Oz* references. The time storm can be compared to the tornado, there's Professor Marvell in *Wizard*, and Ace calls the Doctor – Professor.

The Doctor and Glitz wander round the catacombs which don't seem *very* explored. What are people doing on Iceworld? Is there really treasure here hidden with a stupid, childish map?

We're leading up to **that** cliff-hanger...the Doctor and Glitz encounter a good 'singing tree' set and Mel and Ace get arrested for using nitro nine - they escape via a nice scene with Kane with all the focus on Aldred, so we know she'll be a companion. Only the music lets it down. Any idea what kind of liquid Kane must have in his veins if his blood temperature is at -190 degrees? That's seriously weird biochemistry given that it won't be water. Liquid nitrogen? They encounter what looks like a good dragon mask. Mel screams, Ace doesn't.

Then the Doctor, for reasons no one understands, climbs over a barrier and literally hangs off a cliff.

Part 2 ***

There are frozen mercenaries, stimulating philosophical discussion, a lost umbrella and a dragon for the Doctor to overcome...providing he survives the cliff-hanger – RT (this is the epitome of post-modernism! -Ed)

Based on the in-jokes seen so far one had to assume that the cliff-hanger is a self-referential in joke in a story full of self-referential in-joke but sadly it's not even obvious that it is. As you've read above the director calls it a cock up, but there's still the nagging feeling that it's deliberate, given the Film Studies shtick throughout. I'd bet my house on it, especially given the *Radio Times* preview.

Then Glitz just shows up and rescues the Doctor. Kane sends Glitz's betrayed crew after him, which should be iconic but isn't. Glitz and the Doctor end up on an edge below that definitely wasn't there in the previous episode.

Kane is obsessed with an ice sculpture of one Xana. She must be special, she has no film reference in her name at all!

The Doctor and Glitz get to the Nosferatu. The Doctor distracts the guard at the door with this dialogue:

DOCTOR: Excuse me. What's your attitude towards the nature of existence? For example, do you hold any strong theological opinions?

GUARD: I think you'll find most educated people regard mythical convictions as fundamentally animistic.

DOCTOR: I see. That's a very interesting concept.

GUARD: Personally, I find most experiences border on the existential.

DOCTOR: Well, how do you reconcile that with the empirical critical belief that experience is at the root of all phenomena?

GUARD: I think you'll find that a concept can be philosophically valid even if theologically meaningless.

DOCTOR: So, what you're saying is that before Plato existed, someone had to have the idea of Plato.
(Glitz slips into the docking bay.)

GUARD: Oh, you've no idea what a relief it is for me to have such a stimulating philosophical discussion. There are so few intellectuals about these days. Tell me, what do you think of the assertion that the semiotic thickness of a performed text varies according to the redundancy of auxiliary performance codes?

First, let's remember that Cartmel wrote this scene as an extended joke. Secondly I mean what? Semiotic thickness? Let's try and explains what semiotic thickness is: "Synchronically - at any given point in the performance continuum - theatrical discourse is characterized by the 'density of signs', as noted by Barthes. At each moment the spectator will have to assimilate perceptual data along diverse channels, perhaps conveying identical dramatic information (e.g. simultaneous pictorial and linguistic references to the scene of action) but transmitting different kinds of signal-information. The first characteristic of this discourse is thus its 'semiotic thickness'" from Keir Alam: *The Semiotics of Theatre and Drama* 1980. You see, we can all do this.

And McCoy does seems to be close to giggles throughout the scene. In some ways this is brilliant, but at the same time we cut to Mel and Ace being childish, taking us away from it, and also the two parts of the discussions are not remotely linked. We have a discussion about the nature of existence followed by a quick sentence about performance theory. And yes it would have worked better with another Doctor. I should also add that the Guard's name is Arnheim (Rudolf Arnheim another film theorist and perceptual psychologist specialising in the semiotics of visual arts. Quelle surprise).

Glitz gets on the ship but Belazs is there.

"What are you doing here?" she bellows at the Doctor. "Why is everyone here so interested in metaphysics?" says the Doctor, which I'll grant you is a great line.

"I'll kill you,"

"Ah, an existentialist," quips the Doctor. Another good line, but again it works better with Tom Baker.

The Doctor and Glitz see the dragon and McCoy does some comedy pain as the dragon's laser gun zaps him. Mel twists her ankle badly (as in Langford doesn't act it very well) as they escape the crew zombies, oh dear. Even Ace calls her a doughnut, which is meant to be a term of affection but is less of one on a modern viewing. Ace gets all teary and shares her back story. She's never told anyone her name is Dorothy. Yeah right. Dorothy from *The Wizard of Oz*? Dear me. Yes, whisked off earth to Oz by a storm, just like Ace was.

McCoy's comedy sliding is becoming annoying. They confront Pudovkin (named after Vsevolod Pudovkin a Russian and Soviet film director, screenwriter and actor who developed influential theories of montage. Pudovkin preferred to concentrate on the courage and resilience of individuals, which is ironic as the character here doesn't last long.)

One of Glitz's zombified crew is killed by the dragon and the dragon leads them away. The dragon's head is awesome - the body less so. Clough tried to avoid shooting the legs, quite rightly noting that monster legs always look bad. The dragon leads them to a hologram that gives us Kane and Xana back story. He was a criminal on Proamon and banished to Svartos. The dragon is the treasure 'dragon fire', there's a jewel in it that is the key to the spaceship which is the way back to Svartos. Kane seems to want it very badly…

Part 3 ***

In which Ace and Doughnut run out of Nitro-9, Bazin and McLuhan go after an ANT in the lower sectors and the Doctor finally gets to meet Kane – RT.

Bazin and McLuhan start to prepare to attack the dragon to get the key for Kane. The zombie crew massacre all the people on Iceworld in preparation for leaving. Only the annoying girl survives but in a comedy way. The tone here is desperately wrong.

The dragon starts doing a monster walk. If you don't know what I mean by this may I refer you to *Nightmare of Eden* and the Mandrells. Kane blows up the Nosferatu with all on board, Glitz is devastated. The dragon gets it and Kane confronts Ace. They do a deal and the dragonfire starts up the machines. It's a spaceship but then we find out planet Proamon was obliterated by a supernova years ago. Kane throws a wobbly. In fact Kane melts.

Wait...that doesn't do the effect justice. It's extraordinary. Yes it's lifted from *Raiders of the Lost Ark* but that they have matched it is extraordinary. Mel decides to stay with Glitz. The Doctor doesn't seem to care, well this is based on the way the lines are delivered by McCoy, though they hug. We don't either.

Ace goes with the Doctor after he refuses to let her leave. He has plans, the TARDIS leaves, the little girl watches and grins. The vworp of the TARDIS hustling in the last great era of classic *Doctor Who*...

Verdict:

Well if you go on to read the Virgin New Adventures novels here is the manipulative, game-changing 7th Doctor (played by Sylvester McCoy) making his first move, as he gets Ace and sows the seeds for later encounters. Watched on its own *Doctor Who* fans breathed a huge sigh of relief. This was OK, in fact this was good - relative to everything else this season. In fact it could be argues that if you took out the little girl and McCoy's comedy sliding and it would be rather magical. Haven't said that for a while.

It is still pretty dire by classic *Who* standards, McCoy still feels mis-cast, the music is awful, the tone is wrong, nobody has direction, but the dialogue is being written by people who care and people who get the show. That spine tingling feeling is slowly returning, last seen years ago.

Other famous reviews:

"McCoy gives a ludicrous performance and the production is inconsistent (6/10)" – Episode Guide.

"The kind of entertaining and imaginative serial we hadn't seen for a long time" - Who's Next.

"An interesting attempt to do what *Doctor Who* does best: mix monsters with semiotics and philosophy. It doesn't quite come off, but it's a very useful launch vehicle for Ace (despite some overdone dialogue)" - Discontinuity Guide.

Ratings: 5.07 million: 68th (172)

Position in DWM top 200: 186th (never has a whole season's stories been consistently in the bottom 10% except this one). 215th in 2013.

What have we discovered? The BBC *can* do special effects.

Season 25

Remembrance of the Daleks

One Line Summary: Hi Ben, Andrew here, you know I think you're the best writer ever, after me of course, despite you never having got anything made before and yes I know you've been working on that genius script, thing is…we've got the Daleks so you need to start again…just make it awesome…yes I know we will.

Written by: Ben Aaronovitch - According to the BBC's Caroline Oulton he 'was a fat guy whose mum answers the phone.' Now he's more famous for the *Rivers of London* 'police procedurals with a twist' and perhaps with justification. I prefer Ben's own biography on amazon.com, which I am shamelessly stealing: "Ben Aaronovitch was born in 1964. Discovering in his early twenties that he had precisely one talent, he took up screenwriting at which he was an overnight success. He wrote for *Doctor Who, Casualty* and the world's cheapest ever SF soap opera *Jupiter Moon*. He then wrote for *Virgin's New Adventures* until they pulped all his books.

Then Ben entered a dark time illuminated only by an episode of *Dark Knight*, a book for Big Finish and the highly acclaimed but not-very-well-paying *Blake's 7* Audio dramas.

Trapped in a cycle of disappointment and despair Ben was eventually forced to support his expensive book habit by working for Waterstones as a bookseller. Ironically it was while shelving the works of others that Ben finally saw the light. He would write his own books, he would let prose into his heart and rejoice in the word. Henceforth, subsisting on nothing more than instant coffee and Japanese takeaway, Ben embarked on the epic personal journey that was to lead to *Rivers of London* (or *Midnight Riot* as it is known in the Americas).

Ben Aaronovitch currently resides in London and says that he will leave when they pry his city from his cold dead fingers."

Directed by: Andrew Morgan

Anything else before we start?

Cartmel did his homework during the off-season and watched *The Talons of Weng Chiang* and *The Seeds of Doom*. He noted that yep, playing it seriously was a good idea. *Remembrance of the Daleks* was the story most associated with sowing the seeds for the 'Cartmel Masterplan', which was a term invented by fans and popularised by *Doctor Who Magazine* that described the overall "vision" of this era of the show as seen by Cartmel and his writers. I'll go into this in more detail as we progress, but this is where it is most obvious.

The "plan" according to future writer Marc Platt was "more of a mood and direction" than a detailed scheme. Very little except ambiguous one-liners appear in the broadcast shows but the Virgin New Adventures book range in general (especially the novel *Lungbarrow* in particular) will take it much further. These days those books cannot be considered canon because of the new series' continuity contradictions but for a time they were taken very seriously. My favourite reference to the Cartmel masterplan is actually from *Coronation Street* where fan writers such as Gareth Roberts got the phrase into a script involving Mavis's scheme to retire to the town of Cartmel in Cumbria.

Ben Aaronovitch had submitted an idea to Cartmel on the suggestion of Caroline Oulton at the BBC. She had suggested targeting *Doctor Who*, so he did. He submitted an unsolicited script called *Knight Fall*. To say Cartmel loved it would be an understatement, he writes about 'seams of gold' before he even finished page eight. They became friends and the pair had various discussions about the direction of the show, Aaronovitch becoming the sounding board for many writers of the era. Most of Aaronovitch's *Doctor Who* work, including the Virgin New Adventures books came from these discussions; at the time the most advanced was a storyline that eventually became the New Adventure *Transit.* Then, when Nathan-Turner decided he wanted the Daleks for the 25th season

Aaronovitch had to abandon the *Transit* idea and start again. It would be his first paid writing work.

Cartmel reviewed old Dalek stories and felt only *Destiny of the Daleks* showed the creatures as menacing and decided to use similar shots and shared his ideas with Morgan: shoot low and lots of ceilings. Aaronovitch was therefore told by Cartmel that there must be no capturing and no corridors. The sole Dalek scene at the start was there purely to re-establish the threat. In addition Aaronovitch wanted to re-establish the link that Daleks were a Nazi allegory.

Cartmel remembers reconnoitring the sight for Coal Hill School and seeing it was on Macbeth Street. This disturbed the more luvvie director Andrew Morgan, but didn't perturb Cartmel. He liked the idea of setting it in the year of the first Dalek story was broadcast.

The nickname of the character "Chunky" Gilmour came from a mis-phrase in the script directions – 'Gilmour pulls out his chunky revolver' - which became a bit of an in-joke.

The effects team liked all the explosions seen here, but one modification they made to the Daleks failed; a large orange ball found on wheel barrows in the 1980s was added to the casings to try and prevent wobbling but the actors inside couldn't move their feet. It actually made the Daleks wobblier than they'd ever been. Cartmel was worried that the wobbly Daleks would mean that this would be the memorable thing, not the script. They got away with it - just.

The 'Dalek hit by the baseball bat' scene was iconic but caused more ice between Aldred and Nathan-Turner. Aldred, sensitive to cigarette smoke asked if Nathan-Turner would stop smoking for the next take. Instead he lit up another rather obviously and then blanked her. He also said 'find the camera you dizzy cow' when he watched her on a monitor. He also objected (quite rightly) to Aldred adding badges to her jacket as it caused continuity problems.

The darker Doctor seen here was what McCoy always wanted to do, but Aldred says he defaulted to slapstick because it worked so well for him in the past. Cartmel was also delighted with the transformation of the character of the Doctor, this dark manipulator. Nathan-Turner kicked against it a bit, resisting the Doctor killing Daleks with rocket launchers. When Cartmel objected he said, 'I've let you bend the character of the Doctor as much as I can.'

The Director was going to cut the 'No Irish, no coloureds, no dogs' scene but Aldred and McCoy complained that this was the essence of the piece. This story was about racism. This scene and the sugar cane scene were two of McCoy's favourites. Famously the 'no coloureds' scene was nearly missed by new Head of Drama Mark Shivas when he was shown it. As the scene came up his phone rang and he picked it up, missing the action. Cartmel was furious and insisted the tape be rewound. Shivas thought Ace should have torn up the sign.

Finally, Morgan went over-budget by £13000 so was barred from working on *Doctor Who* again.

Part 1 *****

London, 25 years ago. The Doctor has returned to conclude some unfinished business. Unfortunately some old acquaintances are waiting for him. Ace doesn't like the music in 1963. Wait until she meets the old acquaintances – RT.

In truth there are in very few 'crossing the Rubicon' moments in *Doctor Who*, where the paradigm clearly shifts on-screen. I'd argue we see it at the end of the first episode of *The Daleks*, next perhaps somewhere during Episode 1 of *The War Machines*, or maybe (if we had pictures) the shot of Nanina in a skimpy costume in *The Savages*. *Spearhead from Space* is a given, as is *The Ark in Space*. A less successful paradigm shift is seen in the opening shots of *The Invisible Enemy* when we realised the budget was gone, as was the horror and in came space opera. *The Leisure Hive* is another, although it's probably fairer to say *Full Circle* is the real obvious change.

Then there's *Remembrance of the Daleks*. It's light years away from the mess of the last few years. It feels real, there's mystery and there's a feeling of excitement again. Of course the title gives it away, not the Daleks bit, this is about remembering, nostalgia, despite it only being three years since Daleks were last on our screens. The young Turks run the show now and they want us to be nostalgic. The first five minutes are joyous, as our best loved show, ridiculous and embarrassing for so long gets it so right for the first time in nearly a decade.

The pre-title sequence starts with one of the most awesome shots in *Doctor Who* as we hear the chatter of classic 1960s speeches over an image of the Earth. We get 'Only the pawn in the game' from Bob Dylan – he was a Doctor Who fan so it was easy to get clearance. We also hear De Gaulle, Kennedy and the Duke of Edinburgh (the Queen didn't give permission). Then the giant spaceship comes over.

We see Coal Hill School (hooray!) with one lad in jeans that are bit anachronistic (actually VERY 1980s jeans). It's Chunk Gilmore actor Simon Williams' son. Ace's ghetto blaster is also anachronistic but in a good way. McCoy seems relaxed and...better, Aldred brilliant. A van with an ariel lurks and the Doctor is interested in it. A weird child lurks too. There are also anachronistic cars in a car park in one shot, oops. Even the shot where McCoy gives Ace money is great, despite the best efforts of video tape, bad music and McCoy's occasional lapses into incoherency.

Ace goes to the cafe, and enjoys the fake Elvis on the juke box. The weird girl watching is still the most intriguing thing in *Doctor Who* for ages. 'There's a Doctor at the gate...' was chilling then and chilling now.

In fact it was the first chilling thing in Doctor Who since probably *The Stones of Blood*.

The Doctor investigates nicely and meets Prof Rachel Jensen. There's a soldier 'down' in Totters lane. The scrap yard (where it all started) looks different to its previous two incarnations and it's spelt 'Forman' (wrong it should be 'Foreman'). The Doctor is rather anti-military when 'chunky' Gilmore poo poos the idea of the death caused by a death ray.

"What a predictable response", he snarls. Well does he expect more?

Ace meets another soldier called Mike and she thinks he's cute. Another soldier gets it in the now traditional Dalek way, special effects and a skeleton. It's quite good. Another awesome shot nearly takes out Mike in the van. The Doctor uses Ace's nitro nine and it zaps the Dalek. Err how? The Doctor and Ace are in the van then they change driving places in the tunnel. Errr how? The Doctor says the Daleks want something called the Hand of Omega and says the Dalek they saw was the 'wrong one.'

The Doctor and Ace go to Coal Hill School. There's a grammatical error on the notice board, which would never have been allowed to happen in a 1960s school. No, I'm not going to say what it is! Casting Michael Sheard as the Headmaster was a 1980s masterstroke, although meaningless now. Sheard had played evil Deputy Headmaster Mr Bronson in children's' TV show *Grange Hill* for years so it would

90

have made perfect sense to the viewers. The Doctor is confused for an applicant for the caretaker role, which is lovely continuity to the current series again. As we'll see Moffat really does like this one? Pity the school ties are wrong. They really should have filmed this in black and white.

A friend of Mike's called Ratcliffe takes the Dalek away. He talks to something that looks a bit like Rick Moranis in *Spaceballs* (go look it up, we'll wait for you).

Back at the school the Doctor says he was expecting the Daleks and they're following him, all said in a lovely chemistry lab set. They look down at the playground and see the landing marks of a spaceship - a very small spaceship by the way. Again, the Doctor's explanation for why Ace doesn't remember things ('your species has a capacity of self-deception') is brilliant and still used today. The Doctor describes the thing he has come back for as the Hand of Omega. It's 'very dangerous'. They go down the cellar and find a transmat. A Dalek appears but the Doctor puts it out of phase. Another Dalek appears, white this time. The Doctor gets stuck in the cellar as the Dalek climbs the stairs.

Part 2 ***

London, 1963: the Doctor wants to bury the past – before it buries him... - RT

Of course the Dalek climbing the stairs shot is considered fairly iconic, although clearly Daleks have climbed stairs before (see the Chase in Volume 1). It's less iconic when you realise it was shot with the aid of a Stannah stair lift mind.

Ace rescues the Doctor properly with a shoulder charge to the nasty Headmaster and getting the door open. Outside, the Doctor and Ace admire anti-tank rockets while 1980s vehicles roar past on the road behind - shocking. The Headmaster fixes the transmat; one wonders why Daleks make machines that require human hands and tools. The Dalek attacks from the cellars and the anti-tank weapons work. Again one wonders - how? They didn't in *Dalek* in 2005. The answer is 'for the convenience of the plot'.

Mike's (the soldier Ace fancies) mum runs a boarding house here in London town and he has that slightly Received Pronunciation accent? Is that right? Ace is staying there. Night falls and the Doctor goes to the cafe there's the Butler from *Fresh Prince of Bel Air* is working there! And he's wearing a Christmas jumper! The sugar conversation is rightly praised and it still works. McCoy finally playing it well and beautifully played by James Marcell (as John the café worker) too. There's a lovely sense of time for these scenes full stop.

Another Dalek appears. Ratcliffe talks to a battle computer. Ratcliffe is a racist by the way, actor George Seward doing his Oswald Moseley impression. John Leeson, ex-K9 voice actor makes a brief reappearance here as the battle computer.

The Doctor appears at a funeral directors and shows interest in a big coffin. The coffin moves by itself to an open grave and the Doctor was lucky to choose a blind vicar. This all panders to the fans, but it works. Mike is following the Doctor and the Headmaster appears and attacks Mike. More very modern vehicles and a dog walker go past in the background.

Ace is starting to spot that Mike is an arse. She remains in the boarding house and has a glorious moment with old TV, the racist sign and famously misses the start of *Doctor Who*. This is known as a Meta reference by the way. Of course it's light outside so it's not 5 p.m. in November in the UK and no-one's mentioning Kennedy was shot. Oops, but cute.

Bored Ace sneaks back to the school and has another unlikely battle with a Dalek. The Daleks are all very feeble when it suits the plot. It's a great scene though despite this. The episode ends with her surrounded...

Part 3 ***

Dalek hunting, destruction of the transmat, Machiavellian manipulation, grave robbing, and Ace gets asked to the pictures - RT

Is the graffiti we see around 1960s London a homage to the Dalek graffiti seen in *Dalek Invasion of Earth* or just 1980s graffiti that no-one noticed during filming? Yes, I know what the answer is...don't write in.

Ratcliffe's gang of fascist brownshirts contains a member who is clearly of Afro Caribbean origin: that's ludicrous. I do like that Ratcliffe was originally called Gummer in early versions of the script. John Selwyn Gummer was a member of Margaret Thatcher's government famous for shoving a beef burger down his daughter's mouth to show British beef was safe to eat. It foreshadows the overt Thatcher subtext coming in the next story.

The Doctor saves Ace with a weird electronic device and more Daleks are destroyed. Professor Jensen and the Doctor inspect a Dalek casing. The claw of the Dalek mutant attacking the Doctor is very cool. The open mouth scene less so – cute, but no. Professor Jensen hasn't changed her clothes for today's scenes, although a whole day could have passed. Why script such careful timing earlier to blow it now?

We see the Emperor Dalek, who is hilarious, reminding me of Zippy from *Rainbow* when he speaks. The actor

94

playing the part is Roy Tromelly, and he is going for it. He's a fine actor that Roy!

Ooh, and a quick Quatermass reference too. The 'why do the men call Gilmour Chunky?' line is good from McCoy too. The Doctor tells Ace some Time Lord back-story about the Hand of Omega and Rassilon and the Doctor let's slip a 'we' when he meant 'they.' Oh Andrew you tease us. The Doctor, despite being all-knowing didn't expect two factions of Daleks.

One faction is run by the Rick Moranis figure. The other is run by the Dalek emperor. Luckily for us the Daleks from each faction have chosen different colours to tell them apart. Ah, the Rick Moranis figure is the spooky girl all along. Her controller is one of those plasma balls: oops.

The grey Daleks look very wobbly. Lots of running around and 1980s graffiti on the signs. Mike turns out to be a Dalek rat and Aldred plays her outrage slightly over the top.

The very small Dalek ship lands in the playground. The Doctor 'fourth walls' us and tells us he may have miscalculated.

Part 4 ****

The Omega device is in jeopardy. A giant Dalek warship hangs above the Earth. London has become a battlefield for ruthless alien intelligences – RT

It's just struck me...shouldn't Ian and Barbara be around here somewhere, or certainly missing if set after the first episode. They would be either heavily involved or suspiciously missing. The Doctor's 4th wall antics are cut. Ace, still upset has got a bit attached to Mike. She only met him two days ago. What happened in the guest house? I won't speculate as there's enough debate about Ace's sex life as it is without making the natural assumption of some sort of naughty encounter overnight

Daleks fight each other. It's all a bit static, and then the special weapons Dalek arrives. Now I was at the DWAS Panopticon convention in 1988 when this clip was shown to HUGE cheers. It *was* fantastic, but looking at it in context this special weapons Dalek is no more powerful than nitro 9. So chemicals made by a 16 year old English girl are as powerful as a super Dalek? Please. Good to see the special weapons Dalek back in Capaldi era by the way.

Mike escapes past graffiti clearly saying 1987, oops.

The Hand of Omega is taken to the shuttle and the Imperial Dalek commander proves to be Davros. Should have guessed from the voice: Roy Tromelly indeed. It is of course an anagram of Terry Molloy who played Davros in the previous two outings. Now the anagram is of course to disguise the appearance of Davros from hard-core fans. Why? Any hard-core fan who is watching a new Dalek story is going to be fairly sure that Davros is going to turn up.

The Doctor speaks to the Imperial Dalek. If you don't like this scene imagine Tom Baker doing it. Davros goes off on one and claims the Daleks will take on the Time Lords. How prescient. "Unlimited rice pudding," quips the Doctor. The Doctor plays fear and Davros activates the Omega device and oops it destroys Skaro instead of enhancing it. Skaro is vaporised, just as the Doctor planned. Davros does a runner, Mike is zapped by the creepy girl (eh). Then the Doctor talks the Black Dalek into self-destruction by talking to it. Theoretically awesome but lacking somehow. So it's another "eh?" in the end.

Verdict:

Steven Moffat loves this and you can see why. It is modern *Doctor Who* in all its ways apart from production values, but it could easily be remade now. There's a sassiness to the script we've just not had for years. The girl singing 'there's a Doctor at the gate' still gives me the creeps.

Look, it's a return to form in a big way. The Doctor has his mojo back and he has a companion that does companion things and feels real.

Somehow you get the feeling that there is a plan at last, although perhaps an omnipotent Doctor is a bad idea, and it haunts the show right to the present day.

Nevertheless this sets the scene and at the time it was seen as sure-fire proof that *Doctor Who* was good again but looking at it today there are a lot of flaws. McCoy improves during the shoot but is still too affected and there is a sloppiness to the shoot and the script sometimes, but it's tight and there is a plot spoiled perhaps only by the Doctor knowing what is going to happen.

Flaws abound but this is light years better than *Time and the Rani.*

Other famous reviews:

"The story is undeniably exciting, but it sags under the weight of Dalek Continuity and McCoy is largely incoherent (8/10)" – Episode Guide.

"On the surface it functions as a straightforward *Doctor Who and the Daleks*, but with cool imagery and satisfying battle sequences there's much more going on." – Who's Next.

"The best *Doctor Who* story in some considerable time, *Remembrance of the Daleks* reintroduced mystery and magic into the series with much intelligence and revisionist continuity. *Sounds* magazine thought enough of the story to include *Doctor Who* as one of its 'Reasons to be Alive' in 1989" - Discontinuity Guide.

Ratings: 5.35 million: 86ᵗʰ (194)

Position in DWM top 200: 14ᵗʰ (highest placed McCoy) – moved into the top 10 in the 2013 survey – which makes it slightly over-rated!

What have we discovered? The Doctor is more than just a Time Lord.

The Happiness Patrol

One Line Summary: The one that is so much better on paper, or if you prefer, the camp one, written by someone who isn't camp.

Written by: Graeme Curry - ex professional singer and dabbling writer. He was *Cosmopolitan*'s Young Journalist of the Year in 1982. He had written a play called *Over the Moon* about football, which won a screenplay competition and was adapted for Radio 4. Again he was part of the BBC script development unit and was encouraged to get in touch with Cartmel. You might notice a theme developing. The unit clearly saw a Script Editor who would give green writers a go. This was Curry's first commission, but he went on to write for *Eastenders*.

Directed by: Chris Clough

Anything else before we start?

Cartmel loved *Over the Moon* and wanted to commission something from Curry, but Curry wasn't a science fiction fan and his ideas didn't work. Once again Cartmel handed him a *Halo Jones* graphic novel by Alan Moore (Cartmel considered it to be good science fiction). He also talked about Ray Bradbury's *A Sound of Thunder* (a 1952 story about time travellers changing history by the tiniest of changes) and Malcolm Kohll's *Delta and the Bannermen*, which was in production at the time. Curry liked *Delta* but was warned off aliens and monsters and told to go for something humanoid. Finally, slumped over a chair almost in desperation Curry suggested a planet where everyone is happy and it got the commission. As they knew it would be studio-bound so the idea was to make it look almost deliberately false. They were thinking in the style of Coppola's *One from the Heart* (1982), with its fake skies.

Curry's thoughts were of dreary piped music in lifts and the Americanised 'have a nice day' culture. He originally called it *The Crooked Smile* and Americana was going to pervade the sets but close to production they went for a seedier look. Aaronovitch claims he was involved with a four-day mad rewrite of it, mainly because a planned prison set was deemed too expensive. This is where 'the waiting zone' was invented by Aaronovitch and dialogue about prisons not being needed inserted. The ending was Nathan-Turner and Clough's idea, over the Helen A breakdown finale in Curry's script. The names were thought about to avoid sounding alien. Sigma meaning an alien to the planet.

McCoy claims it was suggested that it was shot in black and white, although it's difficult to know how true it was; he continues to repeat this to this day. He has said his biggest regret was that it wasn't shot in black and white. No doubt the idea was raised but it was more likely to be wishful thinking than a realistic proposition.

The Kandyman is notorious. Weirdly it was given to the costume designer Dorka Nieradzik to design and she made the candy costume. It was nothing like how Curry imagined. The Kandyman was written as a bored sadist in a lab coat and red framed candy glasses. Instead we got Bertie Bassett. Bassett foods complained at the obvious likeness to Bertie Bassett. Cartmel liked the end design, Curry didn't. Cartmel cites Alan Moore again saying *Doctor Who* is best poking into dark nursery corners to justify it – surprise surprise.

This was made first but broadcast second. Cartmel loved the design but felt the usual BBC glare ruined the look. Sheila Hancock playing Helen A only accepted the part so she could play the part like Margaret Thatcher, which brings us to the anti-Thatcher conspiracy associated with this story.

Cartmel said this about politicisation in general: "The idea of bringing politics into *Doctor Who* was deliberate, but we had to do it very quietly and we certainly didn't shout about it. We were a group of politically-motivated people and it seemed the right thing to do. At the time, *Doctor Who* used satire to put political messages out there in the way they used to do in places like Czechoslovakia. Our feeling was that Margaret Thatcher was far more terrifying than any monster that the Doctor had encountered. Those who wanted to see the messages saw them, those who didn't – including one producer – didn't."

Relating specifically to this story Cartmel was a bit coyer: "Well, I didn't see the story as a satire on Thatcherism, but Helen A was a take on Mrs Thatcher, absolutely. Curry says the idea that Thatcher felt her way was the best way and the only way was the inspiration.

"If memory serves, there were three phases. I remember saying to Graeme Curry, 'yeah, yeah, making it an attack on Thatcherism, totally'. Then, of course, we'd soft pedal, saying no, no, of course it's not like that. Then Sheila Hancock, without anybody saying anything to her, totally latched on to it and just played it like Thatcher. So Graeme and Sheila would go to conventions together and someone would ask if *Happiness Patrol* was an attack on Thatcherism and Graeme would feel obliged to waffle for a bit, knowing he might get me into hot water if he said yes, then Sheila would say 'Of course it was!'

"So, of course it was. But nobody intended it to be that and nothing more. We didn't want to produce something that could only function in its period."

Part 1 **

Behind the disturbing façade of Terra Alpha there's an even more disturbing reality – RT

I'm dreading this. It starts with an obvious studio-bound street. A sad woman (a Killjoy) is talked to by a man who is also a Killjoy. No he's not, he's an agent looking to 'out' Killjoys. She's taken away.

The Doctor and Ace arrive. Ace hates the Muzak. Terra Alpha looks empty. Ace claims it's too happy there but the direction doesn't show this, so it seems bizarre. The Doctor has arrived because he's 'heard rumours' and we have the classic 'the Doctor overturns a regime in one night' scenario.

There's Sheila Hancock apparently doing her Maggie Thatcher impression. As foreigners are always given the 'surname' Sigma the Doctor reminds us of his Theta Sigma *Armageddon Factor* nickname – oh dear. Andrew, we *Doctor Who* fans have been trying to forget that ever happened, like the Valeyard.

The police arrest the Doctor and Ace which was the Doctor's plan all along. It's the way to get to the top. Killjoys are banned here, this is Terra Alpha. Another Killjoy fills us in with the sadism of the Kandyman. The Kandy man arrives. It's a bad costume that lumbers. It's excruciating. It's a *Doctor Who* fan's worst nightmare.

The Doctor and Ace steal a buggy, it's very noisy and very slow. A man called Earl Sigma plays the blues and Leslie Dunlop playing Susan Q gives it all. The Doctor meets the man who we know is a baddie, an undercover Killjoy finder. The blues man Earl Sigma helps take him out.

This under populated planet is a brilliant idea just horribly executed. It's meant to be night but looks indoors of course. Better as a planet under a huge dome, but this is never said. It needed a Robert Holmes type to add some stardust, like Hollywood films have script rewriters.

Justin Richards argues that the story is: 'a shell so empty that people have to read non-existent political comment into it in a futile attempt at justification.' I mean theoretically this *is all* horrible. Everybody plays it seriously but it's over-lit and too stagy, but there's something about this...

Part 2 ***

There are no prisons on Terra Alpha, just the Waiting Zone. No executions, just disappearances. And no opposition. But now where is the Doctor? – RT

I mean even the Kandyman has a voice that annoys, but as you watch and listen to its dialogue you realise how sinister it all is. You need to get your head around it. The whole idea is utterly implausible, which means we have to look at this as an allegory, in fact its falseness almost demands it. However this falseness also has the effect of calming McCoy down and he appears rather natural here, which is a good thing.

The Doctor and Earl Sigma walk through candy tunnels and the Doctor warns him from playing notes as it will cause an avalanche: that's foreshadowing you know. The pipe people (underground folk) aren't well realised and they confront the escaping Doctor. They also rescue Ace from captivity. Earl Sigma the blues player isn't playing the harmonica, he's faking. The Doctor calls blues music 'the brandy of the dammed' – woah – it's a misquote from George Bernard Shaw. "Hell is full of musical amateurs: music is the brandy of the damned. May not one lost soul be permitted to abstain?" is the actual quote, I don't think Shaw knew the blues. The Doctor is brought to meet Helen A. McCoy is awesome here. Ace is being chased by Helen a murderous pet. She Nitro 9's it.

Then we have the Doctor meets the snipers scene. And we have that classic line, "You like guns. Pull the trigger end a life. End my life." It's as good a scene as there is in *Doctor Who*. Not plausible, and the gaudy setting doesn't help it, but important. Other lead actors in other eras of the show could have got you punching the air and that doesn't happen here, but it's good to see. Imagine Capaldi doing it. It's the sort of scene we see weekly on the modern show, and it's actually quite rare in the classic era. Colin Baker would have knocked their heads together and quipped.

Ace is to be the star of the Happiness Patrol show and the cliff-hanger is another person dying via a shot of a promo poster being painted over.

Part 3 **

The Blues verses Muzak. Sonnets versus Limericks. The Doctor and Ace versus the Happiness Patrol – RT

This is the most allegorical of *Doctor Who* stories and the English literature types who write about the show go to town on it because of this. It's because it *looks* so false, so it's clearly a set, so it's not real, so therefore it must mean something, there must be subtext. The Thatcher allusions have been dealt with ad nauseum, so I won't go into that now but there are also apartheid notions, with references to the townships and the Pipe People not having the same status. Not only that but what we see on screen pre-empted the essentially bloodless revolutions of the former iron curtain countries about to start in 1989. Finally 'disappearing people' is associated with fascist regimes in South America.

The big one is the gay subtext argument. Essentially Matt 'the Satan pit' Jones wrote an essay about it and *The Gay Times* wrote an article entitled: 'is this the gayest *Doctor Who* story ever?' in summer 2012. And yes, Joseph K and Gilbert M do seem to run off together, but as we've seen above there are SO many other subtexts too. It can't be about all of them can it?

Nevertheless the gay agenda issue is the most well-known and it's worth addressing. Jones' essay appeared in the fanzine *Skaro* issue 7. Entitled 'Tory Alpha: In Search of Queer Nation' it is actually in response to a Paul Cornell comment in a previous edition of the fanzine that the story was an accurate assessment of the destruction of gay rights under Margaret Thatcher. There had then been responses after the initial comment that the story actually wasn't anti-gay enough. Jones' essay admits that on re-watching it and looking at the prose of the novelisation there is not that much 'gay sensibility' (he describes a gay sensibility as liking the sit-com *The Golden Girls*) but concludes that as *The Happiness Patrol* is actually about policing (the clue is in the title) then the way this is portrayed does lend itself to an allegory. The idea of a man pretending to be a Killjoy then revealing he's from the Happiness Patrol is a reference to how police would pretend to be gay to trap other gay people and arrest them. The police are there to maintain 'normality' and the original inhabitants are forced underground (although this really is pushing it). Although towards the end of the essay Jones admits the piece is much more anti-Thatcherism than having a gay subtext he concludes rightly that *The Happiness Patrol* is a celebration of difference, and therefore can be interpreted this way if you want.

I'll say it again, John Nathan-Turner would never have allowed an overt gay subtext in a *Doctor Who* story and Curry said in 2014 that he's happy for people to see the subtext but said it's a bit like the 'Paul is dead' rumours surrounding The Beatles in the 1960s. People find patterns where patterns weren't meant to be.

Anyway…the Doctor laughs hysterically and starts a riot and allows the word *Weltschmerz* to finally arrive in *Doctor Who*. Fifi is poorly realised, its howls don't reflect the glorified glove puppet we see, although it moves well. The Doctor gets a harmonica note to blow up the tunnels, killing Fifi. He then attacks the Kandyman with his oven. Helen A escapes, well tries, but she is betrayed by her husband who leaves with a man – a scene that Curry describers as a way of tying up loose ends, and not what is implied. And the TARDIS has been painted pink. Helen A and the Doctor shout at each other and finally Helen A weeps at the death of her pet.

Verdict:

Interviewed for the DVD Graeme Curry's response to the release was to question why it was being released at all, given how little people liked it. Curry should have had more faith in his own work. There are problems with *The Happiness Patrol*, but they're not weaknesses in vision or approach. They're the effects of a BBC that wasn't up to the job of making drama of this kind anymore, certainly under the title of *Doctor Who*.

It's not brilliant admittedly but it has great dialogue, but so did *The Celestial Toymaker*. Also it suffers from being studio bound, but having said that it has a clearly defined world, it has a sinister villain, and a sadistic executioner. Woah, this is *Vengeance on Varos*! For me, I like realistic *Doctor Who* and this is at the wrong end of the realism spectrum for me, but there is much to admire - the caked white make up, the words.

It doesn't quite work, perhaps because Terra Alpha is too sparsely populated but the end scene from Helen A's perspective where she stands there while the Time Lord judges her, well it's where this mystery Doctor, this interfering champion of time just deals with stuff, and it's great.

If you buy into the McCoy representation of the Doctor then this is the perfect epitome of this Doctor. If you don't like the McCoy era well here you have a lot of evidence for how bad it all was. The Joe Public casual viewers would have found this cartoony take on *Doctor Who* hard to like after the nostalgia fest of the previous story and gave up.

Other famous reviews:

"This odd blend of whimsy and violence has a uniquely run down feel to it – although one can't help wonder if it is by accident or design (5/10)" -Episode Guide.

"A mixed bag of superb elements and lacklustre production values" – Who's Next.

"Still, more than anything else, this is our *Doctor Who* - that which is appropriate to our age and generation. It goes beyond camp into protest. It's not sad, it's angry. And we love it to pieces." - Discontinuity Guide.

Ratings: 5.1 million: 96th (208)

Position in DWM top 200: 170th – 172nd in 2013

What have we discovered? Happiness will prevail.

Silver Nemesis

One Line Summary: How much stuff can we throw into the mix so that people don't notice it's the same story as *Remembrance of the Daleks*?

Written by: Kevin Clarke – Originally from Liverpool he had written two plays and they attracted attention from TV companies. He wrote an episode for the series *Wish me Luck*, and some episodes of police soap *The Bill*, which Cartmel liked and this led to the commission.

Directed by: Chris Clough

Anything else before we start?

Cartmel was a fan of Kevin Clarke's, another novice reluctantly put in contact with *Doctor Who*. Cartmel goes as far as to say Clarke's scripts for *The Bill* were some of the best ever written for British drama, which is perhaps a bit strong. In truth Cartmel let Clarke's solicited script moulder in his in tray for weeks, which meant that he'd left it too late and Clarke wasn't available to write for a year. In that time Clarke spent a lot time in the *Doctor Who* office hanging out with the other writers, all deciding they were the best young writers in Britain. Ian Briggs and Clarke grew particularly close, note the Briggs reference in *Silver Nemesis*: 'I'll return to Briggs his money.'

Eventually Clarke got the 25th anniversary gig. The way Clarke tells it he blagged it by calling the office and saying he had just the thing, then thinking about it on the way over. He lived seven minutes away from Television Centre and so had seven minutes to come up with the idea, whereupon he did what almost anyone would do in this situation and said: "Doctor Who? We don't know who he is." He was a bit bemused that neither Nathan-Turner nor Cartmel knew either. Eventually he summarised the way he saw the Doctor as, "well he's basically God," (and then he claims he saw it all clearly) which terrified Nathan-Turner and Cartmel. Nathan-Turner eventually replied, "Well you can do that but don't say it." What's interesting is that this is precisely how the character is portrayed nowadays.

Clarke was also a fan of *Where Eagles Dare* and other macho movies. All this talk of action movies and the 25th Anniversary desire to bring back the Cybermen, allowed Nathan-Turner to reminisce about the *Attack of the Cybermen* location shoot. "It was so cold we had to tape Nicola Bryant's nipples down, they were obscene." Just so you know.

Of course the idea of putting the mystery back into *Doctor Who* had been around a bit before then. Aaronovitch talks about it as something all the writers had discussed; Briggs called the Time Lords a millstone therefore this story could have been a big part of the Cartmel Masterplan, that recurring thread. This time I'll summarise it the way McCoy did: "It seems that there were three guys, Rassilon, someone else and someone else; a triumvirate, like the holy trinity, who created Gallifreyan society and perhaps the Doctor was one of those.' So perhaps there was a play with revealing who the Doctor was but Cartmel now claims it was all a big tease and it's true that all we get is a wink at the end of this story.

Clarke threw the kitchen sink at the plot as we'll see. This included Courtney Pine, because he wanted to meet him. He also made the Doctor a jazz fan. The 'straight blowing' line refers to clarinet technique (zzzzz). Clarke was also a fan of Jacobean theatre. De Flores is a name check to the servant in the Jacobean play *The Changeling*. He also tried to write all of Lady Peinforte's dialogue in Iambic Pentameter (see *The Crusades* in Volume 1). Clarke makes a cameo in the story too. Now that's what I call everything but the kitchen sink. Aside from this there was the elephant in the room that the story is essentially the same as *Remembrance of the Daleks*, which we'll touch on below. Cartmel seems affronted that people find this a problem.

Many people associated with making this felt the anniversary tag put a lot of weight on a flimsy production; this included the director and McCoy , who felt it was quite good – if it wasn't the 25th anniversary tale.

David Banks, Cyberleader actor and self-proclaimed guardian of the Cybermen back story didn't feel the Cybermen were well served here. "The writer didn't understand the Cybermen, so he used them as a metaphor for Nazis." He also felt that gold had become an angle and they looked weak.

The production seemed to be full of incident; rehearsals were cut short because of the asbestos scare (see *the Greatest show in the Galaxy*) so things were manic. Dolores Grey (apparently famous) left her valuable jewels in a suitcase on the street in London without realising. Anton Diffring playing the Nazi leader De Flores spent most of the time watching Wimbledon tennis on the TV. He was unwell and complaining a lot. I know I just called De Flores a Nazi, of course all actual Nazi references were taken out by Nathan-Turner; they became paramilitaries who just happened to be Germans.

The Windsor Castle scenes were filmed at Arundel Castle in Sussex. Prince Edward was offered a part and Nathan-Turner spent a lot of time working out the correct way to address the letter. Apparently the Prince turned it down but wanted a bigger part

A lot of the extras were Nathan-Turner's friends (Arundel isn't far from Nathan-Turner's home in Brighton – he has a bus named after him these days you know) as he felt it might be his last show. It wasn't. The shoot was rather poisonous, with Nathan-Turner snapping. Cartmel left in a huff, which burst the bubble.

Fiona Walker's (playing Lady Peinforte) first TV role was in *The Keys of Marinus* playing a villainess but I doubt anybody who cast her remembered or knew this. McCoy lamented to an American film crew filming a 'making of...' documentary that he wished they had more time. It's an interesting documentary (it's on You Tube) if only to laugh at the 1980s-ness of it all, especially Gary Downie's cod Jimmy Savile glasses.

It was an Olympic year (1988) and coverage from Seoul ran into October that year. As this needed to be broadcast on 23rd November the running order of the season changed from that originally planned. So you can see Ace is wearing an earring picked up in the next story.

Part 1 **

Exactly 25 years ago today, the first episode of Doctor Who *was transmitted, and children have been watching ever since. Tonight a new adventure anniversary special begins to celebrate the world's longest running science fiction series - RT*

I'm watching the extended version thus giving me 29 minutes of *Nemesis* action. So we get 'the duck' and the Ace painting. Of course there is no commercially available 'original cut' so if you do want to watch it 'as broadcast' you will have to find someone who recorded it and borrow their tape (and their VCR machine).

Twenty-five years for any show is worth celebrating and the opening scenes do feel epic. That could be South America we're looking at there, not a fancy house in the Home Counties. Look, a real parrot that is nearly shot by Anton Diffring, who is definitely *not* a Nazi. Anton Diffring goes on about destiny. He goes on about the 4th Reich: are you sure he's not a Nazi? He's got a bow – pay attention.

We cut to the past and one Lady Peinforte tramps around being a baddie. Oh dear, then we have a bad asteroid/comet model, double oh dear. We move to 1988 and Courtney Pine is playing in a pub garden – yeah right. Ace is interested in Charlton Athletic's results in the newspaper, not the upcoming meteor strike, which is weird because Perivale is in West London and Charlton is in South London. If Ace is genuinely going to follow an obscure football team it's much more likely to be Brentford or QPR, both of which she could walk to from home. Despite the TARDIS crew enjoying the jazz, (the Doctor's a fan all of a sudden); they're shot at and fall into water. We get bad comedy from the leads after escaping. It's falling apart after only eight minutes. A duck appears in the TARDIS and the Doctor and Ace are dry very quickly. The duck was a comedy scene filmed for BBC telethon *Children in Need* and not used. Don't look for subtext.

Back in the past Lady Peinforte and her companion Richard drink a potion that zooms them screaming forward in time to 1988. They land in a Windsor tea shop. Talking of Windsor, the Doctor and

117

Ace go to Windsor Castle to chase the Doctor's alarm (on his machine thing).

The meteor/comet arrives with a bang. The Doctor knows, as he launched it. Wait a minute; this plot is a little familiar. Ace finds the place the bow was and Ace is wearing a fez. How cool! They go back in time to when the Doctor launched the comet. The candles blow out when the TARDIS lands in 1638. Never done that before, now it does it all the time. The Doctor plays with a chess set, is this a Fenric reference? No!!! THERE'S NO PLAN, but if you want to see a plan then go for it. Yes, I know it's mentioned in *The Curse of Fenric* but that's afterwards. That's ret-conning.

The Doctor talks about the statue made of living metal. Policeman near the comet are overcome by fumes. The Doctor and Ace try to meet the Queen. McCoy puts on silly specs and they escape the bodyguards. Ace sees a picture of herself – no-one has ever really explained this.

The Germans non-Nazis secure the comet. It has a statue in it. The Doctor explains that the statue needs the bow (which de Flores has) and the arrow (which Lady Peinforte has) to give control of planets. I'll say it again…wait a minute, this plot is a little familiar. They're about to be shot when the Cybermen show up to allow McCoy to say 'Cybermen' with disgust as the credits roll.

Part 2 **

The Doctor and Ace confront a Jacobean sorceress, renegade Nazis and a very special foe from the past – RT

So Part 1 was OK even if the tone was wrong, but this starts with nothing much happening except for macho posturing on location and the moment is lost. I remember at the time thinking the effects were good but now - no. The Cybermen recognise the Doctor (err how?) and a huge gun battle ensues. The Cybermen look very shiny! There are lots of classic cars at the location - well I thought they were classic cars until I remembered this was made 25 years old. Those cars are contemporary. Then it struck me, this feels modern, the cars took me out of my spell.

Lady Peinforte arrows can kill Cybermen. The arrows have gold tips. Oh dear, this is getting silly and now it's mis-step city as Richard does the comedy 'pray to God' routine and promises to return Briggs his money. This is the in-reference to Ian Briggs – we're in the era of the scene that celebrates itself... Some commentators say Peinforte and Richard are like a Holmesian double act – they're not.

In Arundel, I mean Windsor Lady Peinforte wanders around. In truth Windsor's one of the few towns where they could walk around in period costume and no-one would care. Two skinheads follow them. The skinheads spout the stupidest dialogue ever and get easily outfought and tied up off-screen by Peinforte and Richard. The line from their rescuers: "Who did this?" "Social workers" is considered great dialogue by Cartmel and his writers in the 'scene that celebrates itself'. It really isn't!

The Doctor and Ace escape back in time with an arrow stuck in the TARDIS (a can of worms re impregnability). In the past the Doctor burns a bit of paper and finds a chess set. More Cartmel masterplan foreshadowing to Fenric, especially as Ace is scared of the place for no reason, or just random?

The Cybermen take the comet. Validium the living metal is Time Lord technology that escaped from Gallifrey and the Doctor did something about it: I'll say it again…is this plot a little familiar?

The statue emerges from the comet. The Doctor jams Cybermen radio signals with taped jazz just so more jazz can be in the programme. Novice writers. The terrain around Windsor looks a bit too hilly.

In Peinforte's tomb Peinforte gets hammy looking for the statue but the Cybermen have hidden it in the coffin. The Cybermen seem to have Robomen protecting their ship dressed in very 1989 casuals. Ace blows up the cybership with nitro 9 and admittedly the scene where the Doctor asks if she has made any is one of the best scenes in this era.

De Flores speaks to the Cybermen in terms of Wagner. The Cybermen are insulted, which seems a little emotional. And while we're at it if you were a race that could create whole cyber bodies wouldn't getting immune to gold be a major priority? Anyway, they agree to divide the planet up between them. The Cybermen want the statue because it is 1988, says the Doctor and then notes the 25 year orbit. Every time it returns 1913 1938 there's trouble - except there isn't, as many commentators have noted. The statue seems to arrive *before* trouble!

Back at the tomb De Flores has all the cards, the statue, the arrow and the gold. The statue looks great, Anton Diffring looks breathless (he was unwell), the Cybermen double cross them. And neither have the bow The Doctor can't find the cyber fleet on the scanner then spots a very uncamouflaged and very un-indigenous lizard and realises the fleet is cloaked...and the realisation effect is quite well done.

Part 3 ***

Ace is in a battle to the death with the Cybermen while the Doctor tries to restore Nemesis to where it belongs… - RT

The Doctor has the bow. De Flores is double crossed by his soldiers for no apparent reason. The comm channels lose the jazz via a plot device. The Doctor sets off the statue and does a lot of calculations on what looks like a smart phone. That's why it looks contemporary.

Dolores Grey turns up doing her best impression of 1980s Dynasty-style glamour. Then the Cybermen

121

attack Ace. They all miss (of course) and Ace makes one shot with her catapult and nails a Cybermen twice and causes an explosion, with gold. Although this is dumb it's cool to watch and well shot. The rest are taken out by weedy rocket jets. The statue destroys the cyber fleet.

"Doctor who? Have you ever wondered where he came from?" says Peinforte to Ace and the prickles rub up the spine The Doctor looks tense but it's a damp squib. Richard kills the Cyberleader; Peinforte goes crazy, screams and leaps in with the statue. Back in 1638 Ace asks the Doctor who he is and points out the plot similarities to the Dalek story too. We're left with a wink…

Verdict:

If you're any kind of fan of this era of the show you are well aware of the self-aggrandising nature of the script editor and the young writers associated with the show. Cartmel often goes on about how he was sitting in the room with the best three writers in the country, which is almost funny in its hubris.

Where are these 'best writers in the UK' now? Cartmel has been out of television for ten years and writes the occasional novel and article in DWM about his time on the show. Aaronovitch has carved himself a niche as a novelist, which is good. Briggs is now in theatre management and marketing. Clarke did have a goodish career but hasn't written anything for television for nearly ten years. Marc Platt seems to churn out Big Finish plays. Admittedly Wyatt and Rona Munro have had goodish careers. My point is that they were all very young and needed an eminence gris to oversee them a bit. There is too much in-joking in their work, too excited by getting a commission rather than focussing on the point of the thing.

Silver Nemesis is good example of how their hubris got the better of them because the writing wasn't quite as well-crafted as they like to think. This era is associated with a lot of zingy one liners but narrative clarity is often lost. So *Silver Nemesis* like a lot of stories of the era is a mess in terms of both narrative and plot and how it could have got to the stage where it has the same plot as one previously filmed is disturbing. That is what script editors are for Andrew! And with Nathan-Turner obsessed with getting Prince Edward in it he missed it too. It's a disaster.

Having said that on a superficial level this is the most enjoyable Seventh Doctor tale so far. It's knockabout, cartoony and looks good. Of course plot-wise it's barmy and this is despite it being the same as *Remembrance*. The Germans are obvious, the Cybermen are obvious and Peinforte makes no sense at all, as in she is given no real screen time to explain how she can be so powerful and evil. It's not the worst McCoy but it falls between the two famous allegorical studio-based ones and the four-part blockbusters it's really not very fondly remembered. This is a shame because it should at least be remembered for being the one where McCoy and Alfred are finally quite good.

Other famous reviews:

"The story's all over the shop but the action scenes are terrific (3/10)" – Episode Guide.

"A decent first episode leads to an insipid run-around with lots of padding" - Who's Next.

"A bit of a mess, really. Some passable scenes, but the story lacks pace and character involvement. Its plot is virtually identical to *Remembrance of the Daleks* only two stories previously (even Ace says 'Just like you nailed the Daleks')" – Discontinuity Guide.

Ratings: 5.5 million: 89th (202)

Position in DWM top 200: 176th (206th in 2013)

What have we discovered? The 'scene that celebrates itself' at its peak.

The Greatest Show in the Galaxy

One Line Summary: As tepid 1990's new laddism-drenched joke book *Doctor Who: The Completely Useless Encyclopaedia* had it: "Asbestos: harmful substance discovered at BBC Television Centre in 1988. The team were forced to leave the building and film (this) in a tent, resulting in a more suspenseful and realistic production than had been intended."

(No, no I can't let it go. *Doctor Who: The Completely Useless Encyclopaedia* is a classic example of 1990s Virgin Publishing's output. They knew we'd buy anything with the logo on, but this is truly awful, with one entry being 'Peri's tits'. You think it would be ironic, but it's not - it *is* about Peri's tits. *Loaded* magazine has a lot to answer for).

Written by: Stephen Wyatt

Directed by: Alan Wareing - he came to the profession via amateur theatre and joined the BBC in a lowly position working his way up to the directors' course (as ever). He had worked on *Doctor Who* before, as a Production Assistant on *The Keeper of Traken* and *Timelash*.

Anything else before we start?

This was the story that Cartmel called his watershed moment. He meant it mainly with respect to his own attitude to the show. He felt he finally had the elements in place and so worried less about the realisation; therefore he focussed on producing the best scripts possible. In reality this meant he became more critical of the finished product when it didn't realise the ambition in the script.

The idea came via Nathan-Turner (the title came to him first). He thought they could go back to Longleat to film and set something on a fairground, but he went off the idea as he spoke it out loud. Cartmel and Wyatt were relieved, as they thought it was a bad idea. Despite Nathan-Turner withdrawing from the process they were lumbered with the title that Nathan-Turner still loved. Cartmel preferred a circus and got a copy of the 1935 book *Circus of Doctor Lao* by Charles G Finney, although Wyatt was less impressed and the finished serial is nothing like it. McCoy claims the idea came up because of his circus background, he emphasises he doesn't have one, but people think he has. He does have acrobat skills and he wasn't averse to using them. He couldn't juggle however, which caused problems as it was assumed that he could. He learnt fast. The subtext Wyatt actually went for is 'more dead hippy ideals'.

Wyatt had the idea of creatures coming out at night, but this was unworkable. He said it was planned as a studio-bound three-parter with a game show format. Then the brief was changed to a four-parter, with location work and the back stories kicked in. T.P McKenna (famous-ish) was persuaded to play Captain Cook, a character dreamed up by Aaronovitch when he popped into the office. Jessica Martin playing Mags was briefly the brightest female talent on TV, although she was most famous for impressions. The relationship between Mags and the Captain was toned down so that people wouldn't start to question the Doctor and his young companions' relationship. Ask Nathan-Turner! Whizzkid was a piss-take of *Doctor Who* fanboys and good heavens was it bang-on! It wasn't improvised – the character was originally a computer nerd – but it was very close and you can see how in the DWB hating climate Nathan-Turner would have enjoyed it.

First time *Who* director Alan Wareing was scared witless of doing fantasy after his 'gritty' background. The circus design was based on the Jerry Cottle circus, big at the time. The clowns were Wyatt's way of avoiding rubbish lumbering monsters. Ian Reddington as the chief clown must be credited with a lot of the characterisation. The wave, the eyes, the different vocal tones depending on who he was speaking to were all his ideas.

The shoot was plagued with problems. It was so hot on location that Ian Reddington's makeup ran. The hippy bus is probably still in the quarry as they couldn't afford to move it from the quarry after the shoot and they had permission to leave it there. There was never a

127

real big top on location. The front porch was built, and the top seen was a small model shot well and matte effects used. Famously the explosion scene had far more explosives than McCoy was expecting. He was expecting 'air hoses'. He didn't flinch. Afterwards McCoy thought the explosion had ripped the clothes off his back. On location Aldred and Nathan-Turner finally made up after a skittles match between the *Doctor Who* cast and the cast of *Rockcliffe's Babies*. I kid you not.

The big issue with the studio work was the discovery of asbestos at TV centre which meant the studios were out of action. Nathan-Turner brilliantly arranged for the shoot to continue in a marquee put up in the car park. As the remount had to be on BBC grounds the car park at Elstree got the gig and it was filmed in a marquee that looked nothing like a big top. Wareing thought the whole idea sounded ridiculous but it worked in their favour. The floorboards that came with the marquee made it look much more real. The only problem was the noise from the car park, aircraft flying over.

Part 1 ****

What do the psychic circus, a buried robot and an abandoned hippy bus have in common? The Doctor and Ace are about to find out – RT

This is an awesome slow burner just losing one star for the conductor robot.

As the story starts with actor Ricco Ross playing the ringmaster rapping about the greatest show in the galaxy you may have picked up that there were tokenism complaints made about the ethnic minorities portrayed this season. Prior to Season 25 black or brown faces were very rarely seen in *Doctor Who*. This is not a definitive statement but the last ethnic minorities I can remember in *Doctor Who* were: Tony Osoba as Kracauer in *Dragonfire*, then *Mindwarp*, where Tuza was played by Gordon Warnecke, of "Indo-Guyanese and German descent". Nabil Shaban (Middle Eastern origin) was of course also cast as Sil, but was playing a slug. Going back further it's probably Tony Osoba again in *Destiny of the Daleks* and then...nothing. Not one speaking role. Therefore for there to be suddenly six stories in a row (if you include *Dragonfire* and *Battlefield*) with black characters in does seem a little...'ooh we must include them'. What's worse is when you look at the roles. No problem with the character in *Remembrance*, it's a beautiful part played beautifully, but in *The Happiness patrol* Earl Sigma is a blues singer, In *Silver Nemesis*

Courtney Pine is playing himself and here Ricco Ross is playing another song and dance man. You can see why people could get irritated. All I can say is that the lack of black faces in the universe prior to this was the bigger crime than the sudden righting of the wrong. The inclusion of Brigadier Bambera next season goes further in my mind to show that the times were a changing and the tokenism charge is a bit harsh.

Anyway…the action moves to the TARDIS, how novel. We haven't seen it all season, and will only see it one more time. The Doctor is learning to juggle from a book. Rather ironic given the circus is the setting for the next story. Did he know? The book by the way is called *Juggling Klutz*, which was published in 1977 and came with three balls in a net, although sadly these aren't in evidence here. I learnt to juggle from *Blue Peter*, like all good English kids.

Ace has lost her nitro nine, Tom Baker's scarf is draped around her neck and is that Mel's top from *Dragonfire* (yes- Ed)? And just as I was enjoying a rare old-school scene they ruin it by making a juggling ball disappear for no reason. A thing/robot arrives in the TARDIS and advertises the circus on Zeganax. Ace reveals she doesn't like circuses, especially clowns.

Back at the circus a mean motorbike appears ridden by Nord, a hard-case eating a burger. A bloke called Bellboy and a girl called Flowerchild (dead hippy ideals folks) are escaping from the circus but a silent hearse tracks driven by a clown tracks them. This is as awesome as it sounds. Wareing insisted on automatic windows for the hearse in this scene despite the hearse not having them built in. He was right. Bellboy draws off the clowns allowing Flowerchild to escape. He takes Flowerchild's earring as a memento and causing lots of continuity errors (Ace is wearing it in *Silver Nemesis*). Flowerchild gets to an abandoned bus. She gets grabbed by the neck by an unseen thing. It turns out to be a robot bus conductor. Things were going so well. The clowns cart off Bellboy. The girl is dead. Killed by a robot bus conductor with candy man tendencies.

The Doctor and Ace land and encounter Peggy Mount selling fast food. Ace and Doctor eat her food to get into her good books. Aldred clearly hates it. They fail to hitch a lift on Nord's bike, and we get the glorious line, 'I'll do something horrible to your ears' in response.

Then they meet one Captain Cook and Mags from Vulpana - hello? The Doctor can identify tea from the Groz Valley of Melogothon. The Captain thinks Melogothon is overrated but recommends the frozen pits of Overod (yawn) if the Doctor is ever there. A robot buried nearby wakes up and attack Mags. The Captain does nothing about it and Ace has to zap it. They're rubbing in the contrast aren't they?

The Doctor and team find the bus where the girls was zapped and the Doctor zaps the conductor with words. Ace finds Flowerchild's earring which she was wearing last story.

Here comes Gian Sammarco playing a Doctor Who nerd riding that brand new thing in 1988, a box bike. Ian Reddington as the Chief Clown is awesome and will be every time we see him. He owns this.

Mags and the Captain watch Bellboy suffer and Mags screams worse than Bonnie Langford. Ace is reluctant to go in to the circus tent and the episode concludes with an 'are we going in or aren't we?' from her.

Rob Shearman wrote about this episode that the story is the oddest of the 'oddball' stories and this episode's cliff-hanger is the threat that the story might actually start! All true.

Part 2 ****

Ace thinks clowns are creepy...and she's right – RT

The answer to the 'are we going in or what?' question is 'yes' as the Chief Clown beckons them in. The ticket seller's accent veers between Russian, Italian and French and ends up as drama school 'foreign'. She's called Morgana, why doesn't she get a weird name like everyone else? The Chief Clown sees Flower Child's earring on Ace's jacket. This is impressive observation for a male. Put it this way I wouldn't have noticed.

Inside the circus only a nice 1950s family accompany them. "Shut up and eat your popcorn," says Mum: not very 1950s English language I feel, so it is wrong in so many ways. The Doctor tries to interact and is classified as the first act. Ace is scared, the clown grinning behind. Most of the clowns are robots. Bellboy made them all says the Chief Clown - he can repair them. Just awesome.

The Doctor is caught and McCoy's acting lets him down. He is put in a cage with the Captain, Mags and Nord. Ace is chased by the clowns. A character called Deadbeat appears. The Ringmaster and the ticket girl moan about their lot, she has lost her accent. Gian Sammarco arrives interrupting their whinging: he reminds us he's the greatest fan of the circus.

Nord goes to the ring. He does strong man stuff in the ring and gets a score of 9/10, but can't tell jokes - 0/10. Just some cloth is left as he is zapped.

The Doctor and Mags escape with juggling club trickery. Ace is still free in the creepy flowing corridors. She's found by Deadbeat and finds the Chief Clown, who locks her in the room they store the clown robots, who start to move.

The Doctor and Mags find some ancient stones. Mags doesn't like the crescent sign. They walk along a stone corridor and fine a deep hole. There's an eye looking up. The Captain finds them and tells them the Doctor is next in the ring.

Not once do you think you're in a car park in Elstree. Again, it only loses a star for over-repetition of the rap tune.

Part 3 ***

The Doctor and Ace are trapped in the Psychic Circus battling robot clowns, forces of ancient evil and the most boring human being within three million light years – RT

The Captain is behaving oddly; it's hard to tell whether he's possessed, or simply a way of showing us how someone like the Doctor could be: a travelling bore and a coward. Ace is trapped and panicking, locked in with the clown robots; she meets Bellboy the robot maker rather convolutedly. He gives her a robot controller.

The Doctor escapes when Mags overacts on seeing another crescent. The Doctor meets Deadbeat who's going to show him something. The Captain is next in the ring.

Deadbeat takes the Doctor to Ace, and Bellboy reminds Deadbeat his name used to be Kingpin.

And now we have Gian Sammarco's 'I know it's not as good as it used to be but I'm still terribly interested line' that dogs at all the uber *Doctor Who* fans out there. Firstly it's well played by Sammarco, who has somewhat dropped off the acting map after this: 2) it's hilarious and a brilliant play by the production team, especially in this wonderful little tale. Irrespective of how awful you felt *Doctor Who* was at the time the team were just making a TV show. Fanzines like DWB which had no shame at all about publishing spoilers and using very aggressive tabloid tactics were month-by-month kicking the show. Even the softer official fan club DWAS wasn't exactly friendly, although at this crucial period they had some kind of tax issue and the magazine was barely four pages long. How Nathan-Turner would have loved Whizzkid!

Kingpin used to lead the circus and wanted to bring the circus to Zegonax, but something went wrong when he looked in the well. 'The eye gives you promises heaven or hell' notes the Doctor as he takes Deadbeat back to the well.

We get the goddam rap again. Gian Sammarco goes into the ring instead of the cowardly captain. Guess what...

...Zapped.

Bellboy has stayed behind, the chief clown strikes him (well misses) and then sets the robots on him. His grin and wave to us in the fourth wall is simply marvellous. In fact the whole death scene of Bellboy is gloriously sinister.

Deadbeat recovers his senses as Ace and the Doctor realise how the bus from episode 1 is important. Ace and Kingpin/Deadbeat are going to it. The audience in the big top are getting angry.

The Doctor proposes he, the Captain and Mags go into the ring together. The Doctor saying this will throw a hammer into the works. An old style malapropism or an error by McCoy? In the ring the Captain turns on the lights and makes one of the lights a crescent and Mags turns into a werewolf. The changing effect is not as bad as some say, rather , but McCoy displays horror as disgust which is probably a bad move.

Part 4 ***

The show continues with that old devil moon effect – RT

A little summary for those who have got lost in the plot. The psychic circus was a once wonderful place to be. Kingpin (or Deadbeat) brought the wandering circus here in search of a great power, which drove him crazy. The circus has been under the control of evil gods ever since. To break the spell the centre eye piece of a necklace must be put back, but it is protected in the bus by the conductor (built by the guilt-ridden Bellboy). Ace has gone to get it and the Doctor is playing for time. He didn't bet on a werewolf appearing.

The gods like the werewolf show as T P McKenna's dialogue is covered by the music. The Doctor escapes via a rope swing. But Mags is after him. He confronts the gods. Mags kills the Captain.

At the bus Ace finds the necklace but the conductor is on her. He crushes her head but Kingpin has the eye. It's cap is blown off and it blows up.

The family of the Gods speak in deep voices. They want the Ringmaster etc. The clowns chase after the escaping Mags and also kill the Ringmaster and Morgana. The Doctor goes to confront the gods via a portal. The portal to the gods is a bit poor but give it some slack, it was filmed in a tent. And then we see the real circus ring with the eerie gods of Rrrragnorrrrrock. Pity Gallagher used the word Ragnarock – which is an old Norse word meaning the destruction of the Gods-ish, which kind of gives the game away. If you were Gods would you call yourself this? Apparently the Doctor has fought these gods through time (has he?) and McCoy does that brilliant 'feet nailed to the floor thing' like Michael Jackson in the contemporaneous 'Smooth Criminal' video – the Who team nicked it. The Chief Clown and Deadbeat have a standoff but Ace uses Bellboy's tool to zap the robot clowns, including the Chief.

What is the Doctor doing? It's not clear…

Ace, Mags and Kingpin/Deadbeat take the hearse back to the circus to rescue the Doctor. The gods will do anything to stop them, including resurrecting Captain Cook. Kingpin seems to gets it from the cadaver Cook but doesn't. The eye amulet goes down the well while in the ring the Doctor deflects the gods' energy bolts. The Captain gets it again. The crystal ball blows. The dark circus collapses. The gods die. McCoy walks past a HUGE explosion and doesn't move a muscle, well a teensy blink. The circus blows up with pink smoke. Kingpin and Mags start a new circus.

"You were in control all along," says Ace, which makes no sense, as the Doctor seems to have had this adventure sprung onto him…or did he?

Verdict:

Marvellous of course. There are more ideas (as usual) than a story can handle but at least there's enthusiasm, great design and acting that fits the tone of the piece.

It's a play on 1960s ideals dying where even Ace calls the Doctor an ageing hippy, although this is lost a little in the mix. In the end, like all true great *Doctor Who* it can also be seen as series of great images: the stand-out being the clowns in the hearse. It's mildly irritating to have baddies being 'gods' and the actual premise is barmy if you give it a bit of though. This is adored by the McCoy lovers who made a living writing for the Virgin New Adventures and with some justification.

Other famous reviews:

"Extraordinary images, a cast to die for, great music and narrative that treads the finest of lines between humour and horror (10/10)" - Episode Guide.

"Combines vivid images with a queasy atmosphere that deftly mixes the wacky and the poignant to create a wonderful *Doctor Who* story." – Who's Next.

"A return of chaos, magic and surrealism to *Doctor Who* the story summed up by the scene in which the Doctor walks out of a confrontation amid carnage. Whizz Kid is a (not very subtle) parody of anally retentive, obsessive fans. It could be said that the whole story is a metaphor about the production of *Doctor Who* (Cook = *Star Trek*, the gods = BBC executives, the Chief Clown = Michael Grade, Deadbeat = Blake's 7, etc.) (but it's not – Ed, see *The Happiness Patrol*). The ideas in this, one of the most iconic stories, are very imaginative and the direction is psychedelic." - Discontinuity Guide.

Ratings: 5.43 million: 93rd (205)

Position in DWM top 200: 119th (woefully low, I despair!) – 108th in 2013.

What have we discovered? That Doctor Who nearly is the greatest show in the galaxy again.

Season 26

Battlefield

One Line Summary: You're expectations are sooooooo high and then Angela Bruce says 'Shame.'

Written by: Ben Aaronovitch

Directed by: Michael Kerrigan - Recommended by the now banned for over-spending Andrew Morgan. He had worked on *Knights of God* for ITV and went on to direct *The Famous Five* and *Coronation Street*. In the 2000's he worked on the *Sarah Jane adventures*, making him only the second old skool *Who* artist to work on the new iteration (Graham Harper is the other).

Anything else before we start?

After three years of turning round an ocean liner McCoy finally felt they were getting there, mainly by losing the comedy, or as Cartmel described it: 'the Doctor is a distant mountain range, seen through a mist, an imposing power from a distance.' Cartmel loved the idea of a game playing Doctor who knows all the moves in advance. It's significant that the Doctor's brown jacket makes an appearance here for the first time. As McCoy had been losing the clowning he was known for there was a feeling a darker jacket would help reflect this change. The question mark jumper was never going to go though, it was Nathan-Turner's baby.

This was originally called *Storm over Avallion*, or more jokingly *Quatermass and the Lake*, both of which Cartmel and Aaronovitch still like, but Nathan-Turner felt was too obscure and not punchy. Cartmel would eventually joke it was renamed *Battle Fatigue* as it took two years to get made. Aaronovitch now hates it and can't bear to watch it; he thinks it 'doesn't work as a script, has crappy design and unhelpful music' (Keff McCulloch's last score). He blames himself however and believes putting the Brigadier in was a big error, deliberately ignoring the continuity of *Mawdryn Undead* (well we all want to ignore the continuity of *Mawdryn Undead* – Ed). Aaronovitch claims to have bottled out of killing the Brigadier, although that was the intention, saying 'you've got to be bold,' and then wasn't. Courtney loved the 'get off my world line' – but who doesn't?

As far as the script was concerned Aaronovitch admits he wasn't experienced enough to do what was required, and got away with *Remembrance* somehow. If you have *Doctor Who Magazine #476* it's worth reading his piece on how he'd do it now and you realise this could have been very special. He feels he should have given the best lines to the Doctor and the good lines that were there were just for showing off. Cartmel maintains it's a brilliant script and it still one of his top three stories. One of them is right.

It was originally conceived as a three parter but Cartmel moved it to a four parter and stretched part 2. Aaronovitch's original idea had been about the past coming back to 'bite you on the arse' and then thinking about Arthurian legend and what if the knights were all from a different dimension where magic worked. This is all brilliant stuff but it doesn't come across like this. The idea of the Doctor leaving notes for himself is also a very modern one. The script was influenced by *Quatermass* again and *The Devil Rides Out* by Denis Wheatley. The pentagram scene is almost a direct lift from it.

Cartmel blames the ultimate failure of this story on the design of things like the knights, which were just knights and not knights of the future. Aaronovitch was astonished that designers would go to town on a historical like *Remembrance* but futuristic ones were just knocked together. He was also astonished that Angela Bruce was cast as Bambera because he envisaged the part for someone with a Caribbean accent – hence the 'shame' curse word. "If I'd have known they'd cast someone from Newcastle I'd have changed the dialogue," is Aaronovitch's response.

The thing is I am not sure 'Shame' is any kind of Caribbean swear word anyway. My partner's father is from Jamaica and she has never heard it used as a cuss and she would have done. The concept of 'shame' is an important one in Jamaica, but not in this context, as a curse word. The thing gets weirder and weirder.

Aaronovitch also didn't like the CND speech that Cartmel wrote at the end. It was cut down and Cartmel admits he overwrote it.

Cartmel *did* have an agenda: more Earth-based stories, more humanoid monsters, and less of the TARDIS. Stories would have no connections to previous tales; this came about after the continuity errors of the previous season.

"The TARDIS is great," said Cartmel, "but the less you see of it the better. I particularly disliked people having arguments in their bedrooms in the TARDIS, it was like *Neighbours* with roundels on the wall. The TARDIS is this spooky machine that transports you through time and space and it's bigger on the inside than it is on the outside. But beyond that, it's just a plot device. Sure, it's a cheap set to shoot, but it's terribly brightly lit and looks like a plastic control room. Also you'd get shots of the TARDIS flying through space - why? It's a time machine! I have a kind of revisionist view of the TARDIS."

Aldred loved the location of Rutland water. Marcus Gilbert playing Ancelyn said it was wonderful to be on location because of the long summer evenings, apart from the midges. The 'Ace rising from water with Excalibur' scene was complicated as the water was far shallower than she expected and the sword wouldn't come out of the water straight. If you look you realise how ridiculously close to the shore it is.

James Ellis playing the archaeologist Peter Walmsley felt the part was underwritten and kept adding lines from Tennyson, a lot were cut but a few lines snuck in (go on, spot them!). He also thought the hotel on location was a real hotel and went to bed in a private bedroom.

The helicopter shots had to be done in three hours because that's all the time they had the helicopter for. Alf Joint coordinated stunts and the swordfights. Angela Bruce playing Bambera claims she persuaded him to let her use a sword in that other notorious scene, where a modern Brigadier suddenly decides to use a broadsword and isn't terrible with it. Bruce practised with a pencil. Kerrigan also suggested the fight with Bambera and Ancelyn behind the Doctor. This wasn't choreographed at all. Listen out for the laughing. The car scene with Brigadier and the Doctor took thirteen takes which must have amused Nathan-Turner, acting as the second unit director for the scene.

The special effects went wrong. Aaronovitch cringes at the scene of the Brigadier being blown through a window. But the debris spray didn't happen. Also see the 'Aldred nearly drowning' incident. You can see the clip on YouTube. The glass cracked and broke water flooding onto electrical wires. More on this later.

The Destroyer, undoubtedly one of the best monsters of the classic era, was originally designed to look like a man who transformed into the demon. It was too expensive to do that.

Part 1 ***

England, the near future: the Doctor and Ace join the Brigadier in a battle against warriors from another dimension – and discover that pub prices are outrageous - RT

So this received the lowest ever ratings for an episode of old *Doctor Who*. This is ironic because it was so anticipated by fans. Admittedly the British public were less enamoured and the BBC publicity for this season was virtually zero.

And it starts so lamely with the Brigadier at a garden centre. Courtney is awesome but the writing desperately info dumps. The cut to the new Brigadier Bambera afterwards however is nicely done.

There's a sword in the stone and then we must pause for the last ever internal TARDIS scene, with pictures of roundels not real roundels. Ace is looking a bit glam: earrings, and a top! The Doctor has a new brown jacket. There's a distress signal. They arrive in Earth's future (1995 ha ha). The Bambera spots the Doctor and Ace thumbing a lift. This is all OK and then Bambera the new brigadier says, 'oh shame.' Now to me 'shame' sounds like PG rated way of saying 'shit' but it was meant to be West Indian patois. How wrong is this!? Aaronovitch justifies the line of course, but why give the character an African name if they're supposed to be from the Caribbean? Why not direct Angela Bruce to play the part with patois, or ask her to change it to a curse word she can play convincingly?

Anyway UNIT doesn't stop for the hitchhikers but archaeologist Peter Walmsley. The sword moves to Earth, lands and knights appear out of the ground. This is where Aaronovitch stops watching and I can see why. Director Kerrigan clearly doesn't recognise the futuristic aspect of the Knights; on the DVD documentary he seems more interested in discussing *Henry V*. The music is also pretty bad.

They're filming at Rutland Water, I used to live nearby, quite what a nuclear missile convoy is dong by the lake is beyond me. The Doctor produces UNIT passes for him and Elizabeth Shaw from under his hat. Bambera sends them away but her sidekick Zbigniev knew the Doctor and knows therefore that all hell is about to break loose. Zbigniev looks a little young to have been around when UNIT used the Doctor, irrespective of the weird UNIT dating timeline issues.

The old Brigadier has a huge house for an army man. Courtney to his credit has asked how the Brig could afford such a house (near Denham in Bucks): was it a private income? It's certainly up from the hut he was living in in *Mawdryn Undead*. None of it makes sense at all. Anyway, the Brigadier mentions a King, oh dear, and Doris has never heard of the Doctor - double oh dear. I know a man like the Brigadier understands the Official Secrets Act but really, he's never mentioned the name once to his wife?

Bambera decides to talk to the Doctor and Ace off-camera and they're now all friends. They go to the architectural dig at a nearby hotel. No-one wants the bar man's home brew and a five pound piece is used to pay, oh dear. The Doctor gets interested in a hot scabbard on the wall dug up at the dig. A blind woman thinks it's waiting for something. Bambera finds the TARDIS and various knights fight each other. Then Bambera's Landrover wheel is blown up: 'ah shame,' aaaahh!

Ace and a Chinese girl called Shou Yiung talk explosives, but mix gelignite up with Semtex, which two supposedly expert explosives manufacturers wouldn't do. Again, I'm a chemist by degree: don't let me get started, ok. As Ace says "boom!" (twice in case we missed it) a man is blown through a roof. He's Ancelyn and he calls the Doctor Merlin. And the other Knights appear and want to "Kill them now!"

Part 2 *

The Doctor uses Merlin's mighty powers, the Brigadier discovers a new way of landing a helicopter and Ace goes for a swim – RT

Part of the problem with *Battlefield* is that expectations were so high. It's way better than almost any *Who* of the previous ten years, yet it has a poor reputation. What's really wrong with this era is the falseness of the product: harsh synthetic video tape used on location and harsh synthetic music (McCulloch's last score) means the very good (no seriously, *very* good) ideas here get bashed all over the place. Having said that, this is a terrible episode and it's the one that was expanded to make it a four-part story.

The Earth is centre of a war originating from a different dimension. Mordred (a bad knight) and Ancelyn (a goodie) chew scenery and the Doctor pretends he knows what they talking about - or does he? He's supposed to be sealed in ice caves apparently. Mordred's mother is going to deal with him. No matter how macho you are it's very difficult to deliver a line like that without looking ridiculous. Much as I admire Aaronovitch this is pretty feeble. Bambera and Ancelyn fight in laughably silly circumstances (see above). Back at the pub the hot scabbard is getting antsy. Off it flies into the wall. It's trying to get to the lake.

How far does the Brigadier live from London, he's been in the chopper for hours? Surely a car would be just as quick. And why aren't they in a military chopper? Mordred is summoning something and finding it all rather funny. He's tearing a rip in time and space and the Doctor feels the pain. Now, just in case Mordred's scenery chewing wasn't enough, here's Jean Marsh (ex-1960s companion) playing his mother Morgaine at full throttle. At least these two will make a slightly better fist of the whole historical double act shtick after the Peinforte/Richard attempt in *Silver Nemesis* – won't they?

It's morning; the Doctor is clearing up, Ancelyn and Bambera sleep in chairs next to each other. God, not another rubbish romance? At the archaeological dig Ace finds some runes and the Doctor says they're in his hand witting. Dig here, it says, so it's blows up. There's a tunnel and down they go. The archaeologist seems to be possessed – it's actually the quoting Tennyson ad libs mentioned above.

The Brigadier arrives and Morgaine zaps the chopper. They manage to land before it blows up. The Brigadier meets Morgaine; she doesn't kill him, as he mourns the dead. Nice try Ben.

In the tunnel under the lake the Doctor opens up a door and sort of says he's not Merlin. It's frustrating because we don't know if he's bluffing, which would be cool, or knows it all which is less cool. This ambiguousness is really frustrating. They find Arthur next to the sword on the stone. A rubbish green effect is after them. McCoy still can't do fear. Nice Troughtonesque 'when I say run ...run' riff. Ace contrives to get caught in a trap with the sword and the water is rising behind the glass. It's quite horrible and Ace looks genuinely in trouble.

Part 3 **

The Doctor has gone to the battlefield leaving Ace and Shou Yiung back at the hotel. All they have to worry about there is a demon, nuclear weapons and a witch – RT

It's worth looking at this water stunt because notoriously it went wrong. It was filmed at the end of the day (9.50 p.m.), it was rushed and it was complicated. McCoy is on record as saying he didn't think this it was a good idea to have attempted it with ten minutes of filming time left. Aldred was less bothered because the tank was full of warm water. McCoy says he saw the glass bulge, Aldred says she felt it crack under her hands - the footage is inconclusive. We see no bulge and there is a huge cracking noise as the glass goes, which Aldred legitimately might not have heard in the chamber. McCoy screams, 'shit get her out!' and she's out in seconds. Cartmel calls it Richard Burton-like heroics, which isn't quite true. McCoy was worried she could be electrocuted, or cut. Aldred maintains he saved her life as the water cascaded onto the floor. Kerrigan claims the glass wasn't up to scratch based on the water pressure.

Anyway, this is another horribly uneven episode which cannot get more than two stars because of the pointless racism. There are some great-ish scenes too, but the resolve from the cliff-hanger must go down as one of the stupidest in *Doctor Who* history as the unconscious Doctor simply wakes up and turns off the danger. Ace comes out of the lake holding the sword, which allows some more histrionic acting from Angela Bruce. "LOOK!" she bellows, "IT'S THAT WRETCHED GIRL!" says Walmsley. The Brigadier saves the Doctor.

Mordred drinks beer in the pub being nasty and humiliates the UNIT lass, who is admittedly a bit trigger happy. Her death is one of the most callous in the series, but the reversal of the blindness to pay for the beer by Morgaine is one of the most remarkable. Whether it's good or not is another matter, it could have been directed better.

And while we're praising the production Bambera calling the Citroen 2CV a 'deck chair' is glorious. We've missed good lines in *Doctor Who*. But then all the good work is messed up by the, 'Are you married or what?' line she throws at Ancelyn for no reason. Actually this is becoming a good line fest: the Brigadier's "quartermaster, silver bullets, have we got any' is up there with the classics, but is forgotten. Bessie is unmothballed but has the wrong number plate, 'Who 7' indeed. How did it get here if it took the Brigadier a whole episode to get here by helicopter?

Various shenanigans then Morgaine summons the Destroyer, but we only see it in shadow. He is the waster of worlds, apparently. Ace and Shou Yiung hide inside a chalk circle. They argue and Ace goes down the racist route, which is horribly unacceptable. The Doctor stops the fighting by shouting loudly. Ace won't give

Morgaine Excalibur and we see the blue beast – the Destroyer.

Part 4 **

If the Doctor is Merlin, and Ace is the lady of the lake, where is King Arthur? – RT

The battle scenes I'm sure looked good on set too, but are ridiculous, with men bouncing on unseen trampolines and Bambera fighting with a sword – why? Well we know why, because Angela Bruce fancied it.

It must be noted that the Destroyer is a tremendous effort and it wouldn't look out of place in the modern series. It's the teeth that do it. Yes, the Destroyer looks great but doesn't do much and doesn't sound scary. His chains prevent him destroying the world. The Doctor and Morgaine dance and she releases the Destroyer. Mordred rebels, the Destroyer drools, the Brigadier goes to kill it with silver bullets with a dumb heroic act. 'Get off my world' says the Brig, which is a good line and the bullets work errr how – it's the Destroyer!! And that's the end.

At the site of the king's armour the Doctor receives a note from himself, Ancelyn and Mordred fight with a dumb McCoy walk through. The Doctor prevents Morgaine letting off a nuclear missile by his words. Boom. Mordred and Morgaine are locked up. How is that going to work?

152

Verdict:

Good first episode, terrible second. It falls into the *Timelash* trap of talking about past battles that we haven't seen thus confusing the casual viewer. Let's go into more detail:

What's right with it:

How good is McCoy most of the time? The Destroyer, the ambition, Nicholas Courtney.

What's wrong with it:

Angela Bruce, a fine actress, is miscast, or misdirected as Bambera, which makes the military threat a joke. The bad guys are bad for no reason, which is never helpful. Although a bad example in some ways *The Seeds of Doom* should be watched to see how to do obvious bad guys convincingly. What else? The Arthurian bollocks, the bad costumes, the weak direction and people are having too much fun on location, so the tone is mixed. Bambera is another missed opportunity – so right-on that she almost a PC joke.

On balance it's the biggest turkey of the proper McCoy era. Despite the ambition it just doesn't work. It looks good but a lot of things are there to make a really profound and cool script but not tell a story. There's just no credible threat at any stage and the actors sort of know it's not for real.

Having said that Paul Cornell loves this era of the show and is right when he says it's the best use of the Brigadier, the best monster costumes and laments its revision from classic to dud over the years. Although, as Cartmel and Aaronovitch note it is hard to get past the first few minutes: the knights, 'shame' and the music all blow it.

Other famous reviews:

"Snappy editing aside, this is a confused mess (3/10) – Episode Guide.

"Succumbs to looking overblown and silly" – Who's Next.

"Back in the days when each *Doctor Who* season consisted of half a dozen stories or more it arguably didn't matter too much if the occasional four-parter happened to slip a little below par. In a season of only four stories, however, if one of them turns out to be a disappointment it is a much more serious problem. *Battlefield*, sadly, falls very much into this category. Although by no means the worst season opener the series ever had, it is decidedly lacklustre and a great disappointment after the same writer's excellent *Remembrance of the Daleks* the previous year" - *Doctor*

Who the Television Companion (Howe, Stammers, Walker - Virgin)

Ratings: 3.65 million (the lowest ratings ever). 94th (206)

Position in DWM top 200: 146th (159th in 2013)
What have we discovered? Never try and do 'the near future', or 'the Doctor has a weird future' storylines.

Ghost Light

One-line summary: Yeah right, a one line summary, ha ha ha.

Written by: Marc Platt - Born in Wimbledon in the early 1950s Platt attended catering college before working with Trusthouse Forte hotels. He quit and joined the BBC on the administrative side, involved in the cataloguing the BBC's radio output. He was a big *Doctor Who* fan who had tried to get a story made for years. Finally he found the right script editor…

Directed by: Alan Wareing

Anything else before we start?

As noted, Platt was a fan who got his script made: a very rare occurrence. He had been submitting work to script editors as far back as Robert Holmes but had only received rejection slips, despite his work being deemed impressive. One project actually reached draft stage: *Warmongers*, written with uber fan Jeremy Bentham. It was set in 1940s blitz-torn Britain and featured Sontarans and Rutans (fanboy alert!).

Platt contacted Cartmel with a script called *Shine* relating to stone-headed things in 19th Century Russia. He didn't mention he was a fan, nor that he worked for the BBC, which impressed Cartmel when he found out.

Cartmel said his next effort (*Cat's Cradle*, which became a Virgin New Adventure novel – and fairly unreadable!) had promise too, but was way too ambitious. Aaronovitch (as usual hanging around the office) asked if he'd read Mervyn Peake. When Platt said 'Yes' Aaronovitch replied, "Thought so, he's weird too."

As Platt tells it Cartmel said he'd been working on the history of Gallifrey and hearing about that Platt pitched *Lungbarrow*. Ah, *Lungbarrow*. Again, if you follow the Virgin New Adventures books you'll know this is the last one in the series and worth a fortune on eBay...

Platt but knew the Victorian era well and felt confident doing it in that style. He liked *Alice in Wonderland* and quotes from it extensively and also like the idea of character-driven horror. They worked for eight months on this - the Doctor's personal worst place in the universe - then Nathan-Turner said 'no'. He felt it was too way out and very *Gormanghast* with a sentient house and Time Lords spun from looms. *Ghost Light* developed out of *Lungbarrow*: it being the Doctor's worst place and the house in *Ghost Light* being Ace's worst place in the universe. The murderous housekeeper from Lungbarrow was kept and Platt added Cartmel's ideas about evolution using a few ideas from Doris Lessing's *The Making of the Representative for Planet 8*. Aaronovitch, "the best plot ideas man I've ever known" according to Platt came up with the Manisha backstory.

Josiah Samuel Smith was the main villain and Ian Hogg played it like the great gothic romantics of the era, although he had no idea what the story was about. Platt claims this confusion was deliberate because Cartmel's mantra was that the Doctor always knows what's going on, but here he definitely doesn't. He concedes it's probably too incomprehensible for its own good. There was some explanation in the scenes deleted for time costs and when I say deleted I mean deleted, the BBC deleted the master tapes.

There are allusions including the alien Light's impossible task of cataloguing all life and being driven mad by it as an allegory to Platt's work in the BBC programming index department. A lot was based on William Blake's concepts of innocence and experience. Also, *The Water Babies* was a big influence. Another idea was for Light to be a cosmic version of Victorian naturalists, he would dissect a human just like they would dissect a fly - cue the truly macabre scene where Light has a leg in his hand.

The Neanderthal Nimrod is mockingly named after the great hunter of the bible by Josiah. The idea came from Harry Harrison's *Eden* trilogy, where reptiles rule an alternate Earth and primitive Neanderthal humanoids exist instead of homo sapiens.

Platt wanted Control to be like one of those skinless anatomical diagrams: "too repulsive", said Cartmel. She became a Quasimodo meets Miss Haversham via Dr Doolittle thing under actress Sharon

Duce's command. Control evolves slightly more each time we see her, although you might miss it unless you're told.

The frog and fish footmen heads came from a recent *Alice in Wonderland* production. Platt didn't like them but Nathan-Turner wanted loads of monsters.

The only location work being the establishing shots of Gabriel chase, which were filmed in Weymouth while they were filming *Survival*.

Wareing took the look of Light from the preacher ghost in *Poltergeist 2*, he wanted to emphasise that light was not solid, more a force, which is tricky to realise on a BBC budget and became a glowing aura visual effect. The way round it was to emphasise the cloak and go all pre-Raphaelite.

Nathan-Turner wanted the music score to be played on conventional instruments; something he'd stopped when coming to power, bit it was too expensive, Mark Ayers did his best.

Ghost Light was the last *Doctor Who* story recorded in the old show. Nathan-Turner took a back seat and probably knew it was the end. Gary Downie confirms they found out during the shoot. He felt sad but relieved as he was free from it.

Part 1 *****

Ace tells the Doctor about her worst nightmare and he promptly takes her there - RT

We all know this is a bit of an opinion splitter and before watching it I knew I was going to go 5 stars, or 1, but you can see where I've headed.

An old house with a pink sky painted on with something wild behind a door that likes tea and *The Times* newspaper. We'd better get the explanations out of the way early on. Behind the door is Control. Control is one part of a two-part entity that helps an alien called Light catalogue all life. Control stays in the ship and the Survey Agent goes to the planet to gather data and adapts. They can't exist without the other despite the survey agent's desire to do so. This scene with the tea and *The Times* is the survey agent goading the wildness of Control, although this is very unclear. Nevertheless, this is quirky and dark already.

A grumpy vicar, Reverend Matthews arrives, as do the Doctor and Ace, who's looking very tanned! Ace explores the room they landed in; the Doctor's being casual. Ace thinks it's a Victorian house and doesn't like haunted houses after being in one once. That's foreshadowing folks.

The maids leave at six o'clock and seem relieved to be leaving. A new set of maids appear from behind doors. The Doctor and Ace explore and find a silver box that's radioactive. A big game hunter appears, is shocked at the 'undressed' Ace and says there are atrocities in the house incomparable. He is looking for one Redfers Fenton Cooper.

"Damn tsetse flies," he says when the Geiger counter crackles. A Neanderthal appears and an eye looks through a peep hole. The hunter then goes on about Conan Doyle not believing his stories about giant lizards - a *Lost World* reference and the Doctor asks if the gun he is pointing is Chinese fouling piece (a *Talons of Weng Chiang* reference, although McCoy fluffs it a bit). He sees his reflection and recognises Redfers –it's him. Mad. He's carried away by Sylvia Simms playing Mrs Pritchard the chief maid.

The Reverend is still angry at being ignored. A girl called Gwendolyn appears and placates him. The Neanderthal butler Nimrod invites the Doctor and Ace to meet Josiah. Nimrod is a biblical character associated with the Tower of Babel. The Rev. Mathews thinks the Doctor is Josiah. The niece Gwendolyn takes Ace away to borrow a dress; she's calls her Alice (do I have to?). Josiah turns up wearing inappropriate sunglasses. Rev Mathews is from Mortarhouse College Oxford, made up college based on mortarboards and Porterhouse, a made-up Oxford college in Tom Sharpe's work. Smith talks about moth adaptations as a key facet of evolution. Just in case you haven't worked it out, Josiah is the Survey Agent.

Redfers sits in Gwendolyn's room and fears a bright 'light'. Outside Ace is dressed in 'white tie'. Redfers screams and all hell breaks loose. Ace is pulled away by her hair as she tries to get in. Nimrod calms everyone down and the Doctor's comment is that 'only a madman can see the path clearly through the tangled forest', which sounds like a quote but it isn't. Nimrod goes and works some modern tech and then is attacked.

At the dinner table calf's brains are served as Darwinism is discussed. The phone rings, what year is this? Bit early for a telephone then. Barely nobody had one in England before 1886 and as we'll see this is 1883. Smith answers it seems to say something has escaped, but the language is covered by the music.

Ace finds out this house Gabriel Chase the creepy house from her past - this is Perivale. This is her worst nightmare. She's not happy and she hates it and asks if there are things the Doctor hates: "I can't stand burnt toast. I loathe bus stations. Terrible places, full of lost luggage and lost souls" - lovely from McCoy, who has learned to play the role and he explains what she sensed - evil. Ace gives us backstory about her friend Manisha's house being firebombed and her climbing over the walls into this house.

Josiah Smith comes clean: he has an enemy, the Doctor thinks he's an alien. Ace goes down in a lift. She finds the alien technology. Various dinner jacketed creatures appear...

Over-loud music and weird editing aside this is as extraordinary an episode of *Doctor Who* as there's been. It looks great, it has a lot of logic and cleverness about it, McCoy reins it in and we have something special.

Part 2 ****
The Doctor sees the light and Ace meets some husky friends –
RT

This is messier.

Ace gets carried off by the creatures but Nimrod saves her. It has to be said that the fight does look a little ludicrous. She threatens to break the hi-tech machinery thing and Nimrod is a bit concerned. It breaks anyway. The Doctor goes to help Ace and we have more *Alice in Wonderland* references.

We also get: "Where have you been?" from Ace. And a "Where haven't I been?" from the Doctor, which is surely the first and only *Blackadder* reference in the series. Josiah goes even weirder but the Doctor doesn't think he's the big cheese. The Doctor also explains the husks that are lying around used to be Josiah. He evolves. There's a Beatles 'Hard day's night' reference as Josiah evolves again. I have to say at this point that for the record EVOLUTION DOESN'T WORK THIS WAY MARC!!!!!!

Dawn, a crispy Josiah fires a shot at Queen Victoria. Rev Mathews eats a banana and turns into an ape. The banana is a bit exotic for the 1880s. Josiah finds it hilarious. The Doctor resurrects a police inspector. Ace sleeps and wakes up in bed. As night falls, a gloved hand with the weird voice tries to get out of the lift shaft. We're told it's 1883 and the copper has been in the cupboard since 1881.

"Light will return," is the end of Nimrod's reminiscence, a cowled figure (Control) agrees. What is Light? It's asleep, a very old Nimrod worships it. Nimrod's gone to see a man about a god: glorious. Insects awaken.

The policeman mentions Reading gaol - Oscar Wilde reference, although a bit early. The elevator is a bit unlikely too, the electric elevator was only invented in 1880. Ace finds the husk of Josiah and Lady Pritchard and the daughter. Rev Matthews is still a monkey. At 6 p.m. they wake up, a new Josiah, not scared of Light appears. The Doctor calls on the cowled figure and a rather indistinct woman (Control) to come from the lift and then a bright 'Light' engulfs them all.

Katherine Schlesinger playing Gwendolyn had her name spelt wrong in the credits.

Part 3 ****

Gabriel Chase is an ordinary Victorian house. With a Neanderthal manservant, radioactive silverware and a spaceship in the cellar… - RT

I know the titles in this era always looked crap but next to all this wonderful Victoriana they look even more laughable. Much as the show was having a renaissance the Producer hadn't noticed how the music and everything has failed to live up to the high standards. Could they *really* not afford to use real instruments here?

Light, the alien appears, who's been sleeping. If you're a 'not we' in relation to this story look at Light and imagine how ludicrous he would look without the glow effects. Imagine how the casual viewer (not that any were left) would see this?

Light came to survey the life on this planet but the life kept evolving. McCoy resorts to bad acting again as he tells Light to go. Josiah still has plans for the Empire and hopes the Doctor and Light will be too occupied to notice. Control eats bugs, Light remains confused. Ace is getting freaked by taxidermy. Control makes a run for it through a glass window. Ace struggles.

Light is dismantling a maid - horribly graphic for *Doctor Who*. He holds a severed arm. Light goes on about microbes changing in front of his eyes, which is a little off. Ace tries to civilise Control by quoting the rain in Spain which is from *My Fair Lady*, not *Pygmalion* so it's about 50 years too early to the first film. Then Gwendolyn finds Ace again and there's a fight. I love that Aldred is still wearing Doc Marten boots with her dress.

At dinner Ace is told don't have the soup. The Doctor quotes Douglas Adams' "Earthlings should never invite their ancestors round to dinner."

Sylvia Simms and Gwendolyn turn out to be mother and daughter but Light hates how they've evolved and turns them into stone. This (weep weep) was the last scene filmed on old *Doctor Who*.

The soup turns out to be primordial, the cream of Scotland Yard (get it?), oh dear. Ace confesses to burning the house down. The Doctor talks Light into thinking he's evolved and then quotes lots of Lewis Carroll animals. Light goes a bit loopy and sets off a firestorm program. The tables turn as the ship leaves 'like a passing thought.' Light disperses himself, leaving only a lingering memory for Ace. Ace wishes she'd blown up the house.

Verdict:

It has aged very well because the plot is Moffat-like, it's Victorian so the set designers make it look gorgeous and it's small scale and *Doctor Who* has always worked best when it's Victorian, gorgeous and small scale. Dumb expositions about evolution aside it's wonderful but there's no doubt a teensy bit more explanation would help the casual viewer on first broadcast. The ending, also horribly rushed doesn't help endear it to the viewer either. What we're left with is a series of weird and disturbing images in the true spirit of *Doctor Who*. Remember, the general public only remember things like the giant maggots from Jon Pertwee, not the plots.

The only problem with this is...that it doesn't quite ring true. An all-powerful alien freaked out by evolution is unlikely and Aldred plays her horror as best she can, but it can't really relay that horror too well at tea time, or in 3 parts. This isn't horrific enough, so it doesn't convince. Add this to the often indistinct dialogue and it's no wonder this isn't in the top 10, where it deserves to be.

Platt admits he should have explained more. It's the way his brain works. All the characters are deliberately recognisable Victorian stereotypes - which is why this confuses the viewer because everything else isn't. This is deliberate and in principle a clever twist but, again without warning the viewers at the start it gets lost, or worse dismissed as rubbish.

Cartmel loves this one, calling it the jewel in the crown and *Alice in Wonderland* meets the Marx brothers. Kate Orman says it's 'like having a wave breaking over your head' meaning there's' so much going on all the time. Kim Newnam although not liking much of *Doctor Who* of this era did admit that Katharine Schlesinger in male evening dress singing 'that's the way to the zoo' was good and 'suggested steel under prettiness but sadly the character development was bungled'.

The three single greatest pieces of *Doctor Who* ever? Nearly, but it just isn't loveable, and in truth it's probably a bit too clever for its own good.

Other famous reviews:

"A powerful statement about embracing change is ruined by incomprehensible editing (4/10)" – Episode Guide.

"Smart, funny, subtle, exciting" - Who's Next.

"*The Independent* called this the best *Doctor Who* story in a decade. However, in order to appreciate fully what's going on it is probably necessary to watch *Ghost Light* two or three times. *Ghost Light* is a superb example of Andrew Cartmel's vision for *Doctor Who*. The design is flawless, the direction is beautiful, and the script is a heady mix of the humorous and the macabre" – Discontinuity Guide.

Ratings: 4.1 million: 97th (209)

Position in DWM top 200: 76th – dropped to 80th on the 2013 survey

What have we discovered? Magic.

The Curse of Fenric

One Line Summary: An ancient evil likes to play board games, what next, the Cybermen playing Kerplunk?

Written by: Ian Briggs

Directed by: Nicholas Mallett

Anything else before we start?

The early brief to Briggs was for a historical set thirty minutes from London. Briggs suggested the 1970s, but that wasn't historical enough, so World War Two was suggested, set in Coventry during the Blitz to avoid the London clichés. Cartmel was keen to do another story in the past as he felt these were best realised by the BBC: the World War Two setting seemed obvious. Briggs also pitched the idea of a contest between the Doctor and an ancient foe.

Briggs had learned to be a science fiction fan since *Dragonfire*, although it was a struggle for him. Cartmel said he added science fiction aspects to his stories at a foundation level. As ever, the Alan Moore influence raises its head and this idea came from another conversation about Moore between script writer and editor. Cartmel had read Alan Moore's *Swamp Thing* tale *Still Waters* and suggested aquatic vampires, to Briggs' bemusement. Briggs took this to more obvious literary places than graphic novels and thought about Dracula and the Whitby connection, specifically the North of England as a setting. Once you had Whitby you had the North Sea, which moved Briggs onto Vikings. Briggs had been on holiday in Sweden the summer before and had Vikings on the mind.

The code breaking theme was surprisingly prescient for *Doctor Who*, with Robert Harris's book *Enigma* soon to appear and Alan Turing starting to get the recognition he deserved. Briggs had an interest in the events surrounding the dawn of the computer age, and was eager to make use of this knowledge in light of the time period in which his story would be set. Some sources suggest that Professor Judson and the Ultima machine were conceived as a parallel for Alan Turing and his bombe device - Judson's paraplegia would serve as a metaphor for Turing's persecution; it would also be very gently suggested that Judson and Commander Millington had been involved in a homosexual relationship. While we're on the sex theme, some sources say Briggs had a line about Ace not being a virgin anymore (Briggs' character outline claimed she had slept with Glitz!) but Nathan-Turner vetoed it. The script was ultimately rushed because the schedule was changed and this was filmed first.

With all these aspects the decision to call it *The Curse of Fenric* was made so that viewers would get the theme. It could have been confusing otherwise.

Cartmel and Briggs worked together to make this constantly more interesting, so Russians were chosen instead of Germans to make the baddies were more ambiguous, with the British being the baddies – almost. Setting it out of London helped. Briggs felt he may have nicked the idea of the ancient one from *The Man Who Fell to Earth* but this might be a bit self-depreciating and very tenuous.

Briggs was the man to deal with Ace's emotional hang-ups and he went for it. McCoy felt that sometimes Ace was more important than the Doctor.

Nathan-Turner did not want this to be on location but Mallett insisted. A lot was cut again for timing and 'too scary' reasons: the haemovores were called so not use the word 'vampire', and a slimy death effect was cut unilaterally.

Tomek Bork a Polish actor was hired to play the Russian Captain. He had issues with some of the rather obviously cod Communist lines and had rows with Briggs and Mallet about changing them. Nathan-Turner intervened and placated.

Mallet used two cameras for the final scene with the giant haemovore but someone wiped the tape in one. This was covered up very effectively. He got round it by flipping shots but feels that such a thing shouldn't happen and should be investigated. Mallett felt they had enough material for a fifth episode, although Nathan-Turner contradicted this

No night shooting was allowed for cost reasons, which the designers thought barmy. How can you shoot a vampire story without night shooting, was a typical response? Any similarity to The Sea Devils is coincidental as Briggs would never have seen it and Cartmel assures us he hadn't at the time either.

Ace jumps into the sea because Aldred wanted to do it this season.

If you ignore *The Five Doctors* (and the added *Shada* bits) this took the longest to film. The final overdubs being done seven months after production began.

Cartmel didn't think the director handled the action scenes well and felt the chief haemovore costume was risible.

They had to change the bizarre Ace seduction scene lines because of the inclement weather. The written line "Too hot, the clothes are sticking to me" brought gales of laughter from the crew, who were shivering.

Part 1 ****

The Second World War: the Doctor and Ace visit a top-secret naval base located on the North Yorkshire coast near where Dracula came ashore… - RT

This is a builder episode. Everything is set up, but not much happens, but it gets away with it because it's shot with such confidence. As you watch the opening scenes of Russian soldiers in dinghies with sinister Viking boats sunk below, dry ice helping the atmosphere you realise what a golden era this is. If you grudgingly accept my argument that *Silver Nemesis* isn't that terrible then there hasn't been a rotten, lazy, crappy episode for ages.

The Doctor and Ace land on a 'top secret' naval base. Ace is dressed for the WW2 period. That thing in her hair is a snood – just so you know. The Doctor is wearing the coat actor Sylvester McCoy who plays the Doctor wears on location. And so begins the Doctor's next sick foray into messing with Ace's head…

The Doctor blags past soldiers as the music references 'In the Mood'. He's looking for Dr Judson's office. Once they find Judson (who is in a wheel chair) he is impressed that the Doctor has heard of 'the prisoner's dilemma', a key task in Game Theory. I'm impressed too, as it wasn't developed until 1950. And why Judson is playing around with a cooperation style game is beyond me. That's not going to solve German codes! The Doctor fakes some letter of introduction rather neatly.

The Russians decide to switch to English. None of their Russian accents are convincing, especially the Armenian's, who doesn't look Armenian either. The other dinghies have all disappeared thus explaining the small number of soldiers – not a budget constraint, oh no.

Next day (Sunday?) Ace and the Doctor go to the church. The vicar is Nicholas Parsons. Ace likes some evacuee girls, who have proper London accents compared to Ace's more Drama School one. Down in the crypt is Judson but first we have the extraordinary shot of Millington in the Nazi office. Andrew Morgan has let his hair down this time and gone all auteur.

The Doctor studies translations of the Viking runes as the evacuees swim (they learned to swim where exactly?). Ace doesn't go in with them. This is Maiden's Point, and it's signposted – oops -all signs were taken down in World War Two. Ace and the Doctor meet a young mum with a baby. The baby's name is Audrey, also her mum's name. More foreshadowing folks.

The evacuee girls find military kit, a Russian throws it into the sea. It's caught under the sea by...what? The Doctor and Ace are held at gunpoint by the Russians.

Part 2 ****

The Doctor discovers a secret that's designed to kill - RT

How did those soldiers creep up on the Doctor and Ace without them noticing? They're taken to Captain Sorin. As Judson reads out his translation runes appear in the stone and drowned men wake up under the sea.

The Doctor speaks to a delirious Russian soldier, wrapping his coat around him. Back at the church Millington appears out of a secret passage as Nicholas Parsons reads from St Paul's Letter to the Corinthians in the pulpit of the empty church and stops before he says love.

Millington shows the Doctor and Ace the poisons he's planning to use on the Germans. The Doctor mutters the 'well of hvergelmir' at the sight, which riles Millington. Luckily the Doctor explains for us not immersed in Morse mythology, although the reference isn't entirely accurate, or certainly as linked to the great ash tree, as suggested here. Anyway it seems to befriend them.

Oh, and just in case you thought Briggs had got over his pretentious naming influences, soldiers Prosorov and Vershinin are named after characters in Chekhov's *The Three Sisters*.

Ace talks to the gloomy Rev Wainwright about a lack of hope, as Millington goes to show the Doctor something in the church and they end up at the army base. Eh? Millington shows him the poison in the Ultima machine they hope the Russians will steal. It will go off on the word 'love'.

The London girls go into the sea. Warm water and the fog gets them.

Millington makes the random order to burn all chess sets. Even the Doctor asks if the order is peculiar.

The Ultima machine translates the runes – 'let the chains of Fenric shatter'. The girls turn into long-nailed harpies. Another story you'll hear on the fan grapevine is that Cartmel had a thing for girls with long nails and how they appear regularly, but again, to me it looks like a bit of a coincidence, rather than a thing. More weird is -how the heck did they grow so fast, and did their toe nails grow just as fast? I know, stupid question. The harpies seduce a soldier and monsters grab him under water.

Ace solves the rune logic problem and the old girl gets it from the harpies. They're really scary, although a bit drama school. She's found by the Doctor and Ace randomly blood drained. How?

Out of the sea come the Haemovores, a very effective scene. The Ultima machine is working and making it all happen - thanks Ace you've released Fenric...

Part 3 *****

When the curse of Fenric calls, the dead rise up from the sea...
- RT

Let's be clear, Part 3's are usually fillers, but this one is the exception. It's a cracker.

The radios on the base have been disabled. Would they really do that in a rationed war? It's raining suddenly. Everybody is calling the monsters vampires or Haemovores. Talking of Haemovores, the scene where they march along the beach is hugely effective. Note how Ace never leaves the Doctor's side too – deliberate - to develop the relationship.

Atmospheric shots very *Nightmare on Elm Street* as the Haemovores attack the church. Ace makes it to the roof, scales down the tower and gives us the last ever companion undergarment shot. The Russians save her. The Doctor sends the rest away by muttering his companions names. Close examination reveals he only gets as far as Steven, which is a relief for a number of reasons: 1) it avoids the 'is Katarina a companion?' conundrum 2) the thought that muttering Dodo would keep monsters away would have been a bit silly and far-fetched.

Ace and Captain Sorin seem to have a thing for each other. He uses his faith in Communism to get safe. The monsters cower. The vicar's Bible works on the Haemovores for a bit but he's soon killed.

The script assumes a steamy climate, with a storm coming. The location thought otherwise. Ace calls herself 'not a little girl'. There follows the weirdest seduction scene in *Doctor Who* and possibly in all TV history as Ace talks about a storm coming as she shivers when it should be hot and steamy. Her weirdness gives the Doctor time to free Millington. The Doctor goes on about evil since the dawn of time. The machine spits out a name. Dr. Judson is zapped. Rain pours down and up stands Judson with green eyes and 'we play the contest again Time Lord...'

Part 4 ****

The final moves in a chess game that's been going on for 2000 years. Even if he wins the Doctor may lose – RT

The Doctor and Ace are to be shot for treason – a rather rushed scene. The Doctor needs a chess set. The rain is fake, the sky is blue. The evil girls are summoning a HUGE haemovore out of the sea. Fenric moans about failing to defeat the Doctor's chess move last time. Soldiers gas other soldiers with green gas. In the missile room which looks like a series of breasts (not just me, so did the cast) Ace and Sorin exchange badges, ahhhh.
The giant haemovore is blue, the second blue monster this season. You wait 25 years...

Judson's nurse gets it, everyone is getting it. Ace mentions Gabriel Chase which would have been much cooler if it had been foreshadowing rather than post-shadowing.

The Doctor sets up a chess set. Ace sends the mum and Audrey to stay with her gran. The girls come to get her but they disintegrate horribly as Judson destroys them all.

Millington gets it from a dying Russian, who says the pawns fight together which Ace realises ha ha is the solution. She tells Sorin, who is now Fenric, who loves the pawns. Sorin tells her who her mother is. The Doctor tells Fenric to kill Ace. He mentions chess set in Peinforte's study, he mentions Dragonfire and says he saw Fenric's hand in it all. He gets to Ace. A fire starts. How does the fire start?? (see the production problems above). The serpent rebels. Ace forgives the Doctor, Ace jumps into the sea and comes out cleansed of angst. It's a bad dive. And all is fine and it ends with a laugh ending. Surely not?

Verdict:
Pretty good, but it does have major flaws in narrative, structure and plausibility. However, because everyone, including the viewers knows this is an epic and everyone plays it to their best efforts they get away with it. The wartime setting gives it another boost. Just imagine it made by the 1970s supergroup: Hinchcliffe, Holmes, Maloney, Simpson...

Other famous reviews:

"Hugely atmospheric but the plotting is sometimes cloudy (7/10)" – Episode Guide.

"A revival of the gothic horror stylings of the early Tom Baker years is superbly integrated with the confident new direction under Andrew Cartmel." - Who's Next.

"This is something special." - Discontinuity Guide.

Ratings: 4.1 million: outside the top 100 (217) the lowest position ever.

Position in DWM top 200: 30th – moved to 26th on the 2013 survey.

What have we discovered?: The Doctor knows what's going to happen before having the adventure and Ace goes weird when she fancies someone.

Survival

One Line Summary: Given that this is the last story before the show was axed almost permanently it's the one with the ironic title.

Or... of course, *Revenge of the Care Bears...*

Written by: Rona Munro – a History graduate from Edinburgh University, she had been sent on a BBC writing training course. Cartmel was also there. Cartmel remembers being at a wine and cheese party and most of the guests rolled their eyes when he said what show he worked on, but Munro screamed with delight. This would have been her first paid commission. As a playwright she has since won awards and it could be argued that aside from Douglas Adams she is writer with the highest 'proper' credibility of the classic era, with a series of well-received plays based on King James in the West End, starring Sofie Gråbøl.

Directed by: Alan Wareing

Anything else before we start?

Cartmel liked Munro's sent-in script about child-minders. He rated her because she got science fiction and went to see a play of hers called *The Way to go Home*. Cartmel suggested Munro look at *Tin Tin* comics to get an idea about clear storytelling, which made Munro laugh out loud. She thought *Tin Tin* was a wimp.

Nathan-Turner called this an oddball and wanted the Master in it essentially as a buffer against a new writer – insurance if you will, McCoy said he felt Anthony Ainley (playing the Master properly for the last time) would like to spend the rest of his life being the Master. Munro used the inclusion to explore the relationship, how the Doctor always wins and doesn't care. It must drive the Master mad, which is interesting because Missy in the current series is being written in similar way.

It was originally called *Catflap*, but Cartmel thought it was too tongue in cheek. He regrets not using that title now. Cartmel wrote the final overdubbed line about people made of smoke once they knew it was all over. It was important to leave open the possibility of a return.

McCoy liked it, but felt that it didn't quite work. Cartmel felt the animatronic cat blows it. The animatronic cat was made because there had been a successful animatronic dog in a series called *I Lovett* (a comedy show by a now forgotten comedian). The maker of the dog was brought in. Of course a dog is bigger than a cat and so the design was fatally compromised.

Director Alan Wareing saw the Cheetah People in the script and said fine, as long as we don't get *Puss in Boots*, but as Munro says that's exactly what he got. Regarding the costumes, specifically the cheetah heads.

Ainley said: "I was told that when they put out the tenders, they were brought in, one businessman said 'What do you think of this?' it was wonderful but it was expensive. Another businessman came in with a different cheetah head, said 'What do you think of this?' It wasn't so good, but it was cheap. Of course the BBC took the cheap one. My own feelings on them... this sort of thing shows, and I think it was a little sad. But I hope you liked the cheetah heads you got. At times, they looked quite frightening, but at times they looked like teddy bears, which wasn't the idea."

Munro carried on: "I think the actors that were cast, from what I was told, were doing all this wonderful expressive facial work, and then these *Puss In Boots* things were dropped on them – and so then you can't see what they're doing under there. Particularly Karra and Ace, there were whole amazing scenes between them and for me, that was supposed to be my lesbian subtext – and you can't see it!"

It was another scorcher on location. Gary Downie fired one actor who moaned about the costume and the heat. Big at the time comedy double act Hale and Pace were cast as the shopkeepers, but a lot of their lines were cut.

Ainley waxed on about the make-up and it's so glorious I'm going to quote a lot: "I was put in this chair, I felt captive there, and this man had this thing in his hand and I couldn't believe it was going into my eye. He said 'Lie back, relax' and he did some black magic,

184

and it was in my eye. He said 'Here's a mirror' and I looked and it was wonderful, it looked like a cat's eye with that perpendicular slit that they have, beautiful eyes, and I thought: 'This is going to be magic'. What happened? After a few weeks, they decided that this man wouldn't be with us on filming, we'd have to do it ourselves, so they gave us these little cheap rubber, no slit, contact lenses, and we could put them in ourselves. It took a bit of practice. Quite nasty. I was disappointed, because they just looked like yellow eyes, they didn't look like cats' eyes.

"The teeth, I had to put fangs in. I didn't want to, but I was told to. I went to an orthodontist, and they put in these fangs, with a bit of plasticine, but I found it very hard to speak, very hard to speak clearly, so I took the bottom ones out after a while. Bad continuity, you might notice that, but they got in my way.

"In the fight with Sylvester, I accidentally hit him quite hard with a large bone. I didn't mean to hit him. These things are done by numbers, and you work it all out, and somehow I managed to hit his wrist very hard with a femur, that's a large bone. Sylvester, having had to wear those wretched contact lenses that day, didn't like it, because he hadn't had the training (with the lenses) that Sophie and I had, and he was finding it very painful to put them in. He didn't have much help. He wasn't enjoying it at all, he was in pain, and when I hit him on the wrist with the bone, I said 'I'm terribly sorry', he said 'It's okay Ant, I'm now in so much pain in my wrist, I can't feel the pain in my eyes'.

There was a dispute between normal stunt-man Tip Tipping and Eddie Kidd a famous stunt motorcyclist. Sounds like a union thing. Kidd was riding one of the bikes at the end.

Munro wanted to give Cartmel the ammunition to keep this wonderful show alive but felt she wasn't up to the task. Both Cartmel and Munro agree that if they had known this would be the last broadcast story of classic *Doctor Who* they would have done something very different.

Part 1 ***

The Doctor takes Ace on a sentimental journey to her old neighbourhood, only to find something nasty is stalking the streets of Perivale – RT

I've always loved *Survival* so forgive my bias, although it's the idea rather than the realisation - the boring Sunday scenes in Perivale are very effective; the animatronic cat is crap though - especially the ears. Lovely early shot though and cats running everywhere. This was actually filmed in Perivale. Scenes like the cat fight are so un*Doctor Who*. Oh dear, the Master appears to be directing the animatronic kitling.

The Doctor and Ace can't find any of her old friends, so they go to the youth club. There's a self-defence class running. Sergeant Patterson makes our first mention of 'Survival of the fittest', immediately followed by the Doctor. The 'Cats' poster on the wall is a brilliant addition - by McCoy. Ace tries the pub and the Doctor find Hale and Pace running a shop. We get a third 'survival'... reference. There's a cat hiding in the tins. Tiger, Hale and Pace's dead cat doesn't look very real either. Ace picks up the wrong black cat as the Doctor uses cat food to lure the real black kitling.

Ace is stalked by a giant cheetah on a horse in a playground. It's effective in this scene and Ace is zapped to a quarry. Wow. The Doctor's frustration is great too. On the planet the sky is pink. The cheetahs go for you if you run. She meets Shreela and the old gang. The Doctor and Paterson are zapped to the planet and the Doctor bumps into the Master in a tent...

Part 2 ***

The Hunting World is a dangerous place. The Cheetah People may track you, hunt you and kill you, but that's not the danger – RT

Much has been made of themes in this story. You know the female changes at certain times of the month. It's not something Munro or Cartmel discussed in interviews and it's easy to put this down to another *Happiness Patrol* gay subtext thing. I mean if this had been written by a man would they have discussed menstruation? The main scene that theorists use is the one where the blood red sun reflects off the lake as Ace drinks from it and starts to change into a wild scary cheetah person.

Anyway…I love Paterson's karate gesticulations as the Cheetah people take them to the Master. Ace galvanises the losers of her gang and is determined to capture a Cheetah using the old rope across the road trick - no chance. The Doctor and Paterson chat on their horse as the planet groans. The humans attack the Cheetah people with rubber rocks. McCoy is glorious here shouting at everyone to calm down and tripping some up with a hat raise. The Master describes how the cheetah people fighting causes the planets destruction (not in the original script and not really needed).

The Master needs the Doctor's help. He's trapped and is turning into a cheetah. Ainley fakes a howl. Ace seems to be taken over by the planet, so is her friend Midge. Midge is sent back to Earth with the Master and Ace's eyes turn yellow. It's all a bit earnest.

Part 3 ***

The Doctor and Ace move towards the final confrontation with the animal inside us all – RT

One thing to point out here is how brilliant the music is in this story. It's by Dominic Glynn and its stand-out instrument is the Pink Floyd-like electric guitar work on the score. Yes, guitar, almost the first time the instrument is used in *Doctor Who,* and they only got away with it because Glynn hired the guitarist while Nathan-Turner was on holiday.

Paterson wishes he had a gun but the Doctor points out things would be much worse as the violence would escalate. The scenes where Ace and the Cheetah girl run in slow motion are quite unlike anything we've seen in *Doctor Who* before.

Back on Earth the scene where the Master and Midge are in a suburban house is another beauty. The Master berates Midge for giving in and plays up his will power.

Ace is fighting the contamination and nearly chows down on a corpse but somehow she resists. Anyone want to explain that? The humans hold hands and they go all go back to Earth. Ace and the Doctor look for Midge and find a hilarious dead cat.

Midge gets a motorbike and goes to self-defence class instead of the sergeant. A little girl called Squeak, Midge's sister, tells Ace and the Doctor about Midge and the 'bad man'. It's Adele Silva in her first acting role. She had a reasonable C list career after this: soap operas and reality shows, oh and appearances in men's magazines in her underwear. Where did it all go wrong?

Ace gets her yellow eyes back but that helps them find the Master and Midge. Sergeant Paterson is killed by Midge and off we go to Horsenden hill for a very long motorbike scene. Midge arrives on a bike so why is there another one there? McCoy gets on the handily left bike. They charge at each other and there's a huge explosion. Weirdly cartoon. Midge appears to die. Where's the Doctor??

Ace can't fight the boys and Karra appears to save her. The Master kills Karra with a blunt horn, she turns into Lisa Bowerman, the Master and gives us his last ever Muttley laugh. Ace is sad and a cheetah person takes back the body.

The Doctor landed on a mattress and survived. The Doctor and the Master have a fight and end up back on the planet. The Doctor's eyes change and they fight. "If we fight like animals we die like animals," he screams and he's back on Earth. Again - what?

The Doctor and Ace go back and the Doctor says the last obviously dubbed-on lines after 694 episodes. "There are worlds out there where the sky is burning where the seas asleep and the rivers dream people made of smoke and cities made of song somewhere there's danger somewhere there's injustice and somewhere else the teas getting cold. Come on Ace, we've got work to do."

Verdict:

Well I thought I loved it but actually it's a little too silly to be taken seriously. Quite how the whole thing is supposed to work is beyond me and there are too many scenes where you go 'wait a minute' and you lose the concept. Part one is actually rather good, but the next is a bit of a run-around with the dying planet added (by Cartmel), and Part three although tying things up, does have a lot of very dumb scenes.

Despite this there's a lot to admire; Aldred is great as is making Perivale eerie, Ainley has rarely been better but there's a lot of stupidity too and on balance this is actually one of the weaker McCoy stories. What holds it together and separates it from the less favoured Season 24 stories is McCoy playing it properly and holding it together, something you couldn't have said two years previously.

Kim Newman felt the last sentence "Come on Ace we've got work to do" was interesting, as the Doctor had never felt that saving the universe was work before. He then implied that as the series had become a chore for everyone maybe the word should stand.

Other famous reviews:

"A beautifully written story dealing with big themes in an adult way (9/10)" – Episode Guide.

"Proof positive that *Doctor Who* could be worthwhile, beautiful, powerful and strange right to the end" - Who's Next.

"*Survival* is another very good story, which strikes just the right balance between genuinely funny off-beat humour and compelling drama." - The Handbook

Ratings: 4.9 million: 92nd (204)

Position in DWM top 200: 80th – goes up one place to 79th in the 2013 survey.

What have we discovered?
That *Doctor Who* is no more...

What happened next?

Season 27

It's ironic that after ten years of *Doctor Who* desperately scrabbling around to get any writers for the show in 1989 Cartmel had only four slots a season and lots of good writers. Therefore there was optimism for the future. McCoy claimed that the last series had no press because Nathan-Turner was saving it all for his (Nathan-Turner's) departure announcement. He fully intended to go this time. Nathan-Turner was offered *Bergerac* but turned it down. He regretted it for the rest of his life.

Was Season 27 planned? Musician Mark Ayres swears there was a wrap party after *Ghost Light* and everyone said 'see you next year,' however McCoy was told by Nathan-Turner that it wasn't coming back. Peter Cregeen, Head of Series at the BBC at the time wrote a statement in December 1989 reassuring fans there would be a longer gap but hoped it will be successful in the 1990s. Of course the BBC managers had learnt their lesson from 1985 and Nathan-Turner didn't have the fight left. Cregeen felt a lot of shows had run a long time and they needed to be looked at seriously.

So Nathan-Turner got his wish and left the show but never worked for the BBC as a producer again. He effectively became a custodian of the *Doctor Who* brand.

Cartmel felt the show was deliberately killed by bad scheduling . Aaronovitch felt the BBC was run by people who hated science fiction, who were Oxbridge graduates who hated the scorn of their peers. McCoy felt the powers that be were bored with it.

Colin Brake, another BBC writer felt being on *Doctor Who* was a career killer at the time and the drama department weren't proud of it. Brake was asked by Cregeen who should produce *Doctor Who* and Brake couldn't believe they had no idea what to do with it. Cregeen says they decided it wasn't the show it had been and needed a long rest. Cregeen claims that had there been a clear vision for reinvention from someone, but I feel it was very low on its list of priorities but he swore it would be back in three years' time.

Cartmel got an offer from *Casualty* and took it because of the limbo. Aaronovitch says he was never offered Script Editor but Cartmel wanted him. Cartmel also talked to Colin Brake, who *was* a fan of the show and apparently the only other person likely to have been offered it?

McCoy would have done one more season but no more with the new producer. Aaronovitch said, let's do historicals, the deigners do a good job with historicals but nothing was nailed down. There were more vague ideas.

For example: *Earth Aid*, involving the Metatraxi insane warrior insects set as a space station space opera. It would have discussed the politics of food aid through a mad science fiction filter. Ace would have been in the captain's chair of a huge ship. The Doctor's in her cabin saying 'this is not gonna work.' Big ideas but Aaronovitch knew the design would be bad. Another idea was *Ice Time* – where they wanted to use the Ice Warriors in an *Avengers*-style late 1960s piece. This story would have written Ace out and Ace would go on to train to become a Time Lord to inject new vigour to the old boys. The new companion complete opposite of Ace. A gangster's daughter who went straight, an aristocratic cat burglar. See the *Planet of the Dead* for how this might have worked. Beyond that there was little planned, but this isn't surprising as the show was always recommisoned late.

The Virgin New Adventures

Doctor Who didn't die of course. For many fans the series effectively continued in the Virgin New Adventures series of novels. These books appeared sort of monthly for the next five or so years. It's important to appreciate how influential and important these books are. If you want a longer look may I guide you toward Lars Pearson's *I Who* series (Mad Norwegian Press) for the definitive look at the books.

The early books were written either by old hands from the Target range, Terrance Dicks, Nigel Robinson and John Peel but also a lot of TV writers rejected ideas appeared in the series at various points: so Marc Platt's

Time's Crucible and *Lungbarrow* became novels, as did Aaronovitch's early ideas in the form of *Transit*. Cartmel also wrote three books for the series.

The real breakthrough was with the fourth book written: *Timewyrm: Revelation* written by Paul Cornell. The previous three books had been regular almost pulp *Who* fiction but this story of a church on the moon was so out there and brilliant that it turned the series on its head. From then on the series commissioned many authors new to writing and many of the ideas and themes in the modern series started to appear. It really did sow the seeds of modern *Who*. So, aside from Cornell, Matt Jones, Russell T Davies, Gareth Roberts, Mark Gatiss and Steven Moffat (in a short story) all make their debuts here. More importantly many of the ideas here were grabbed for the new show, and one story completely re-written. Their influence is incalculable.

So the Seventh Doctor although having a truncated and messy TV life turned into the most adventurous and interesting of the Doctors in the hands of people who really love the Doctor.

A few Virgin New Adventure Reviews

A few years ago I wrote a number of retrospective reviews of some of the Virgin New Adventures line for the DWAS magazine Celestial Toyroom. I have reproduced the first four below, pertaining to the four *Timewyrm* Series. If there is a strong desire by the readers for the rest of the series to be reviewed let me know via twitter and I'll consider it for Volume 8.

Timewyrm: Genesys – a Retrospective

Twenty-five years ago this book had a lot riding on it. It promised more adult adventures, 'stories broader and deeper than possible on television'. It was also hoped that the New Adventures would bring in readers new to *Doctor Who* while keeping the established fans happy. For such an important book, editor Peter Darvill-Evans chose a man with only three Target adaptations to his name and no published track record of creating his own fiction: very brave.

Considering how important this book was: the first ever New Adventure and the survival of *Doctor Who* outside of television resting on its shoulders, its insignificance today is rather surprising. Where it is mentioned it is almost universally criticised. As a story I think this is a shame. Where I am in complete agreement with the critics is in the actual realisation of the book.

Firstly the sheer weight of what it is asked to do almost buries it. Peel was obviously told to re-introduce everything so that new readers could be drawn in. This means giving us great chunks of nonsense in the introductory chapters about the Doctor accidentally erasing Ace's memories and even drags the 4th Doctor back in to help. It doesn't work at all; in fact I can almost see all those new readers giving up in droves. When I read my first ever *Doctor Who* book (*The Monster of Peladon* – hardly anyone's first choice) I had no idea about any *Who* background and I needed no gimmicks to draw me in; the idea of a man in a time machine having adventures was enough. They would have been better ignoring the past completely and just getting on with the story.

This brings me to the realisation of the book. One of the paradoxes of the New Adventures and their authors is that writing a novel is far harder than writing a script. Yet the New Adventures editors commissioned an awful lot of untried writers to tell their stories. A writer of a *Who* TV adventure only has to write basic stage instructions and dialogue. A Script Editor will hone the script, a designer will add further creative ideas, the director will have an input and the actors bring in the reaction, the emotion. An author of a novel has to do all this alone and when it's done well you don't notice it being done. When it's done badly however novel writing is very hard work.

John Peel's inexperience is rather noticeable here. His first error is in failing to nail either the 7th Doctor or Ace's character. The 7th Doctor here is an overly chatty small man with an umbrella and nothing more. Ace is merely a streetwise teenage cockney with an interest in explosives. Ace is so one dimensional sometimes that even though she must have been travelling with the Doctor for some time now, with all the Fenric trauma behind her, she seems not to have been changed by it at all. Surely she would have learned to talk with less contemporary slang to people not from 1980's London by now?

Worse is Peel's almost amateurish lack of viewpoint, or head popping as it's more colloquially known. Pick up any modern novel (ignoring Bernard Cornwell's Sharpe novels – an exception always proves the rule) and it adheres to a limited use of a point of view in a scene, or in a whole book. Whether its first person singular (I did this and that), or the third person where we get into the heads of various characters there are rules that shouldn't be broken if you want to create readable fiction. You need to avoid chopping and changing viewpoint in various scenes. In technical terms Peel wrote this book (probably unintentionally) using an omniscient viewpoint. This is the way it was done in the 19th Century, flitting from one character's thoughts to another in the same paragraph. Unfortunately this constantly shifting viewpoint does not expose the reader to any character long enough for us to identify with them. The reader lacks intimacy with the characters and it feels like no-one is telling the story. A strong editor would have sent the first draft back and ordered a change. The story could have been told using only Ace, En Gula's, the Timewyrm and perhaps Enkidu's viewpoint. Gilgamesh has so few thoughts of his own that we don't need to be in his head at all and I always prefer it when we don't know what the Doctor is thinking. This viewpoint confusion is at its worse in the scene at the start of Chapter 10 when in the space of four pages Peel changes viewpoint ten times. The reader's head is reeling at the end as he is almost pulled in and out of the various characters. The whole scene could have been seen through Ace's eyes.

Add to this rather over done dialogue, (Peel isn't sure if he is writing for laughs or not), and characters that have only one dimension and we end up with a reading experience which gives us very little to cling to emotionally. Peel also gives a bit too much away as he writes, telegraphing the Timewyrm's intentions so the reader gets it before the Doctor – another cardinal sin (especially with the 7th Doctor).

All this is a shame as the Mesopotamian setting is novel, although again Peel is rather keen to show us how much research he has done and ignoring more important narrative aspects, like giving us a sense of time between the long journeys in the book. He makes the cities of Kish and Uruk seems to be about half mile apart when they are nearer 100 miles. The story itself isn't too bad, a little bit 'Talons' a little bit 'Time Warrior'. The Timewyrm here is rather fun – kind of an updated cyberman with emotions and modern computer technology. And I love the idea that the Doctor's attempts to destroy the Timewyrm actually cause her to become an almost unstoppable being which the Doctor is forced to chase and try and destroy. Unfortunately this rare *Who* scene of the Doctor making a mistake is ruined again by a pointless comedy cameo from the third Doctor which takes your eye off the plot.

So *Genesys* is a bit of a disaster and it needn't have been, the editor has to take the blame. The biggest irony is that were *Genesys* remade as a TV adventure it would probably be far more coherent, interesting, atmospheric and well-received than it was as a novel. That's a tremendous criticism of a New Adventure.

Timewyrm: Exodus – a Retrospective

I hate interfering with history stories. Verity Lambert got it right by avoiding real events in her historicals, using them and famous characters just as a backdrop to a good story and laying down (an admittedly flawed) rule about not 'being able to change history, not one line'.

Of course if time travel *is* possible then interference in the timeline is also completely possible and in the *Doctor Who* universe the Doctor interferes everywhere in every story ever made. I have never been able to fully accept the double standards of the Doctor's tremendous desire to avoid the corruption of the Earth timeline with anything happening before the present day but having little or no interest in protecting timelines of other planets, or indeed any in the Earth's future. Surely the Doctor knows the future 'official' Earth's course of events as well as he knows the past because, in principle it's all in the past to a time traveller. In conclusion, if the Doctor spends his entire 'career' interfering in history, then any story based on changing history and the Doctor trying to *preserve* it is on very dodgy ground, because if you start thinking about this too hard then the whole idea of Doctor Who falls apart and that is a bad thing.

Exodus is an interference story and takes the form of a quick read by the old master of the Target range, Terrance Dicks. He's a good pro Terrance, his descriptions in the Target books are legendary; in fact they are so legendary that *reviewers* of Dicks books have also started to use the same clichés when describing him. Getting Dicks involved with the New Adventures range was an obvious move, as his name was well-known, (reviewer cliché coming up) and he provided a safe pair of hands. He does a very professional job here without doing anything new. He nails the Doctor and Ace's characters perfectly from their first appearance, he writes with style and the story zips along: you have to turn the page. Apart from these style points though we are on dodgy ground.

The Doctor and Ace land in post-war Britain to find that the Germans won the war. Determined to find the source of the interference the Doctor and Ace go back to various points in Hitler's life to work out where things are being manipulated. They find not one alien race involved but two...which makes the whole thing immediately rather implausible.

Firstly, isn't it a shame that the Timewyrm in the title has clearly been bolted onto this sequel to *The War Games* rather belatedly and how writers are already bored with her. She probably occupies less than ten pages of this book; she remains trapped in Adolf Hitler's mind for the entire story. The real baddies here are the War Chief and the War Lord and unfortunately they come across as a totally incompetent pair of buffoons, losing even more credibility when in the denouement they admit that their previous plan (in *The War Games*) was pretty stupid as well. At this point I could almost visualise Dicks himself shaking his head in disbelief as he wrote the words.

Time hasn't done the book any favours either. Since *Exodus* was published there has been a resurgence in Nazi stories and quite a few Nazi 'what if they'd won' books have been published. So Robert Harris' *Fatherland* and Stephen Fry's *Making History* have become part of our culture and this does not really stand up to comparison to the chilling worlds created in these books. This is a shame as Dicks did his research well, weaving the plot around real incidents in Hitler's life and hinging the plot around his inexplicable indecision before Dunkirk which cost him the war.

I have problems with the editing too. In the previous story that chronologically immediately preceded this one (*Genesys*) Ace had no concerns at all about being understood by people from Earth's past, and even went as far as to speak to Mesopotamians in modern 'estuaryesque' English. In this story she has real concerns about being understood by people from Earth's past, when she worries about not being able to speak German. Did the editor read these books at all?

My final moan is that Dicks breaks the fundamental rule of Who stories and ignores the 'crucible' plot device. The early Who stories used the TARDIS as simply a machine to get the travellers from one story to the next. The TARDIS was usually disabled early on in the story so that the travellers could not simply nip back into the TARDIS when things got a bit rough. Here Dicks ignores this and has the Doctor summon the TARDIS to them at crucial points in the story so that they can escape. This is shocking and again I could imagine Dicks feeling very guilty as he wrote the words. He even gets Ace to vocalise this guilt by pointing out to the Doctor how stupid it is.

So *Timewyrm: Exodus* scores well for entertainment but scores poorly for quality. The New Adventures have yet to take off.

Timewyrm: Apocalypse – a Retrospective

In DWM 305 a 'reader of the New Adventures slush pile' revealed the ten most common mistakes found in Doctor Who submissions. As most of these seemed to cover the first two stories of Timewyrm series – most obviously 'the continuity packed plot' – those War Games are back again, 'the wildly inappropriate setting' –Nazi Germany – it is rather fitting that another slush pile no-no, the 'deadly dull' story comes next. Harsh? It's the common opinion of a book often reviewed using phrases like 'it's the kind of book which one can remember nothing about a day or two after finishing reading it.'

Nigel Robinson was a former editor of the Target range, famous for novelising the Hartnell stories no one else wanted to write. I recall that he used the word "Time Lord" rather incongruously with the 1st Doctor, and every story he wrote seemed to contain a belching reference that certainly wasn't in the original scripts. He was another safe pair of hands, but as with Peel's earlier Genesys, here is another writer with no background in creating original Who. I didn't read this book first time around (I read it for this article); I don't know why, but I guess that a poor cover, uninspiring blurb on the back (saying the characters in the book are essentially boring doesn't help) and probably dashing off to read Revelation, as it was the last part of the series and one always wants to know what happens. This book is asking to be skipped over actually, and even some of the characters elect to do so. The Timewyrm's pawn Hemmings introduced in Exodus doesn't re-appear until *Revelation*, after being stolen away at the end of Exodus in a rather strange coda to that book. The Timewyrm, like the Master in Season Eight, seemingly has no faith in her own dastardly plots and has a number of evil schemes in the pipeline should one fail. Shame really as she appeared to have spent a lot of effort on this one, as it required about 5000 years, some very dangerous timeline intervention into the Doctor's past and serious amounts of genetic manipulation to get the Apocalypse plan into action, yet Hemmings' non-appearance tells us none of it is important to her.

I shall avoiding spending too much time on the rather silly plot. With the 'boring' perfect people being controlled by telepathic aliens, who in turn are ruled by the Grand Matriarch, who the second Doctor met when she was a young girl in a rather convenient 'Face of Evil', *Timelash* plot devicey sort of way. Anyway the Timewyrm is really the Grand Matriarch and she has been persuading the aliens to take cells from every species in the universe (does this include bacteria, trees, wombats and rabbits?) creating a new species, selecting the most talented and 'distilling' the best into the 'God Machine' – which will be so powerful that it will be able to save the universe from dying. Yes, I know that this clearly wouldn't work and so does the Timewyrm. She really wants to God Machine to use as a powerful tool to have mastery over time and space. Unfortunately this perfect entity has no aggression and Ace is needed to supply that. Now I'm no Charles Darwin but if there's one thing living things need to survive it's aggression and it seems strange that this wasn't 'distilled' from the cells of every living species. So it all seems rather badly thought through. What also strikes me as really strange is that this all-powerful Wyrm needs to go to all the trouble of breeding a new life form. Surely such a creature would have mastered some kind of genetic engineering and could have done the whole thing in a couple of hours in a test tube.

As for the quality of the writing it is clear that the *New Adventures* still had no idea what they wanted from these more adult stories. Robinson tells a very conventional Who story here but in an attempt for it to be seen as more adult he includes some rather gruesome descriptions as if this was all adult literature was about. The characters are so bland as to be almost non-existent, and those that do exist seem to have been created from some kind of off-the-shelf Doctor Who character generating kit. Also, Robinson seems to make it up as he goes along. There is no foreshadowing at all, action points suddenly occur with no real reason to except to fill a gap. The classic example is the sea monster in Chapter 16, which suddenly attacks Ace and her companions on a hovercraft. No problem with a surprise attack of course but the reader expects to be aware that hazards exist. The segment reads: "Having trailed them since they left the harbour, the sea lizard excitedly following the trail of fresh blood, had chosen this moment to strike". And the reader says 'what lizard? What fresh blood?' The 'the' implies we should have read about this lizard before but this is first time it has been described.

There are numerous examples of this and the book is tough to get through because you don't care enough to turn the page. This is a shame because the end scenes are quite good, with Ace showing the first time her frustration with the Doctor's game playing and using of people to win.

Still great change was just around the corner. Here the Doctor and companion walk away from the story at the end leaving the planet to recover alone, and dismissing them from their minds. In the very next book this lack of conscience would be blown away forever. In the next book *Doctor Who* changed forever and the New Adventures took off at last.

Timewyrm: Revelation – a Retrospective

This is the fork in the road. This is the book where you either decided to continue buying the Virgin books or you gave up on them completely. It must have been *Revelation* that did it because there was nothing in the first three books to rouse any emotions at all in a Doctor Who fan. *Revelation* however was so radically different to anything before that you either punched the air and screamed 'at last!', or you got very angry and muttered about where 'proper' *Doctor Who* had gone. At the time I was in the latter category but that was my problem. Like many fans I had become so interested in the show that I bogged myself down with obsessive ideas about continuity, Time Lords and sequels to past triumphs. The show was stale and fandom had become a scene that celebrated itself and the show's producer listened to the fans. I can now see how we fans of the programme ultimately stifled the show completely but at the time *Revelation* seemed utterly un-Whoish. Now I believe that *Revelation* is why we've still got stacks of new *Who* product every month. It's that important.

Firstly, the style of the prose is so different. Cornell writes with an almost feminine feel for the emotions in his characters, but he was also a *Doctor Who* fan and all *Doctor Who* fans wanted the show to be seen as serious adult drama. So Cornell did as a fan writer what no professional writer who happened to write for *Doctor Who* would have ever considered doing at the time: he wrote an adult book. Consider this simple line early in the book: "Neither of the Hutchingses were religious, but in a towny sort of way Emily had thoughts that the local church was the best way to integrate with the local community". In the history of *Doctor Who* there had never been a passage like that! It so beautifully describes Emily Hutchings, you know exactly what sort of woman she is but I suspect any child reading the book would get absolutely nothing from it at all. Once you've read that line you know you are somewhere new. It's adult, it's intelligent and it's written by someone who needs to tell this story and not by someone looking forward to the royalty cheque.

What else is important about *Revelation*? It's unfilmable and is the first New Adventure to be too broad and deep for the small screen. It deals with the character of the Doctor and what makes him tick. What is going through the mind of this person who has seen so much evil and so much death? How does a man who can have thirteen different personalities in a lifetime hold onto his sanity at all? This was radical stuff at the time. I'm still not entirely comfortable with it if I'm honest, but somebody needed to do it. Unfortunately this introspective style was taken up by other writers who take 'Time's Champion' and fight the universe and muck about with things from the television show.

This is also the book where science detached itself a little from the Doctor's adventures. In the past, especially the Pertwee years, Kit Pedler and Christopher H Bidmead's work there was scientific explanation somewhere there, even if it was babble. Here there are attempts to explain things but it is lost under the sheer size of the enemies the Doctor faces. From now on it seems the Doctor is battling Gods and superbeings to whom normal laws of the universe do not exist and the Doctor exists on the same playing field. *Doctor Who* as a place where you might learn a little was disappearing.

I wouldn't say *Revelation* was an enjoyable read. It unsettles you, Chad Boyle the bully of Ace's childhood comes back to torture Ace and child evil has always unsettled me since I read Lord of the Flies. Hemmings' return from Exodus is less well done as the cartoony character Dicks created doesn't quite work here. The Timewyrm is back with a vengeance after hardly being around at all in the last two books. She is repulsive and very powerful, Cornell cleverly shortening her name to 'the Wyrm' to emphasise her evil. The fact that not much actually happens that isn't a dream means that you can get a little lost in what *is* actually happening as Cornell adds more and more layers of imagery onto the story. The book itself starts well, with some high spots (the dance with Death, the mistletoe in the mince pie) then it drifts under its own weight for a while before the ending picks up again, but as Cornell himself admits this was his first book and at the time he wasn't good at putting his good set pieces together. He would get better but even so, with this book he changed the way we look at *Doctor Who* forever.

Love and War

Fandom amused itself in the 1990s by looking at old *Who* stories and laying into them in an ironic, post-modern sort of way. Many of those responsible for this also wrote Virgin New Adventures. Twenty-years on I wondered how some of these stories have stood up to the test of time. Paul Cornell's *Love and War* seemed an obvious place to start, as it pretty much placed the New Adventures into a world of their own. It's the story where Ace leaves the Doctor for the first time and the Doctor meets his definitive novel companion Professor Bernice Summerfield.

The Doctor and Ace land on Heaven, the Doctor apparently there to look for a book. The Doctor concludes (knew) that the Hoothi had infected the planet and will soon re-animate all the dead flesh buried on the planet, and as Heaven is the place where Draconians and Humans bury their dead, there's a lot of dead flesh about. The Doctor pretends there is nothing that can be done, knowing that Jan, Ace's new love will take matters into his own hands, dying in the process. Ace leaves, screaming 'get me away from him!'

The story itself is pretty good, very readable, with a nice twist on the 'leave for love' companion departure, but if you look deeper at this story it is just *The Ark in Space* re-written on a huge scale, budget unlimited and horror content turned up to eleven. There is a great imagination at work here however; the Hoothi are horrific, as is the way the infest planet 'Heaven', but it's still the *Ark in Space*! For Noah's self-sacrifice to destroy the Wirrn read the Doctor's nudging of Jan consciousness to destroy the Hoothi. And while we're on the subject, isn't it a little convenient for Jan to be able to produce mini-fires from his body? Reminds me a little of the much ridiculed Hexachromite gas cop-out in

Warriors of the Deep. Admittedly Cornell hides it better, making it 'cooler', but nevertheless it's the same trick.

'Coolness' pervades this work. As you are probably aware, a Doctor Who fan rarely admits his obsession with any degree of pride, knowing that what we love about the show cannot be found by the uninitiated who only see the Myrka, the rat in *Talons* and the Kandyman. The New Adventures writers were always trying to be cool, trying too hard, I think, eventually leading Lawrence Miles to parody them all in *Christmas on a Rational Planet* with his chapter "Obligatory chapter named after a pop song". Almost half of *Love and War's* chapters are named after pop songs, with the occasional film reference (*Heaven's Gate*) too. Was this done to impress non-cool *Doctor Who* fans to make us realise that, hey being a *Who* fan is cool after all? Or was it to show casual readers how cool *Who* is? Then there are Ace's cultural references. Now I know this is cheap hind-sighting, but Cornell is guilty of this in *The Discontinuity Guide* so he's fair game, but the thought of intergalactic new age travellers still playing *Golden Green*, a rather feeble raggle-taggle number by the Wonder Stuff, seems fairly ludicrous. I doubt the lead singer of the Wonder Stuff even remembers the chords now in 2003, let alone Jan's band 500 years into the future on a far distant planet. The Levellers, the Waterboys maybe (no, not even then) but not the Wonder Stuff. And I do have issues with Ace being a fan of Kingmaker, wearing one of their T-shirts when she wanted to impress Jan. They were terrible Ace! And why was Ace listening to this music anyway? It was all recorded a few years after she left Earth, which was probably in 1986 (according to Cornell's own *Discontinuity Guide)*! Kingmaker didn't release a record until 1992 and *Golden Green* wasn't written until 1988. Did she get some tapes sent to her in Iceworld? Does the TARDIS hold hoards of forgettable late 20th century music? I think the Smiths would be more feasible for Ace to listen to but what do I know.

Yes these are cheap shots and I don't really mind these attempts to make Ace seem like a regular girl but when Cornell then drops in Johnny Chess, a fictional pop star the whole thing just grates. You can't mix 'hip' cultural references and then an unhip made-up one.

Another irritating part of the book is the appearance of the character 'Paul Magrs', whose name you may know as an author of some of the BBC range of Who books. Now of course at the time he wasn't 'famous' but now the name stands out horribly and brings you out of the story with a jolt. I am sure many the New Adventures writers put their friends in the books, it's a shame really.

And another thing! The 7th Doctor's 'time's champion' persona here has gone too far. Even during the televised adventures it seemed a bizarre way of bringing back the mystery to the character. Surely a lead character who knows the answers at the start removes some of the interest in the character? This, of course, is not Cornell's fault as it is an extension of the television guidelines, but he is the author who really pushed the envelope here. What with throwaway dream paragraphs where the Doctor talks to Death about how he 'killed' his 6th incarnation, and the innocent book the Doctor wanted to find that just happens to contain all the answers to the problem of Heaven. It's lazy; is the omnipotent seventh Doctor any more mysterious than the 'I'll explain later' sixth doctor? No! Call me a traditionalist but surely a Doctor who arrives somewhere unknown, didn't plan to go there and has to use his brain to solve the problem is more interesting. Having 'seen something like it before' is lazy too and this entire culture of referencing the past probably killed the show in the end.

Cornell should be given credit for Benny Summerfield. She's sexy ballsy, academic and human and she gives the Doctor much more scope for solving problems using his brain. She's promising here and she'll just get better and better. Not sure about her extensive knowledge of late 20th century British culture ringing true but I'll let it pass as it makes her even more likeable.

So *Love and War* reads well and does the job but it's not the masterpiece it's supposed to be. It could have been a lot better had Cornell not been such a fan of the show and all that cringey hipness could be edited out.

Also available

Doctor Who: Episode-by-Episode – Volumes 1-6